Nicolas De Crécy
Glacial Period

ComicsLit   LOUVRE
                 éditions

ISBN: 978-1-56163-855-0
©Futuropolis/Musee du Louvre Editions 2005
©2006 NBM for the English translation
Translation by Joe Johnson
Lettering by Ortho
Printed in China

2nd edition, June 2014

ComicsLit is an imprint
and trademark of

NANTIER • BEALL • MINOUSTCHINE
Publishing inc.
new york

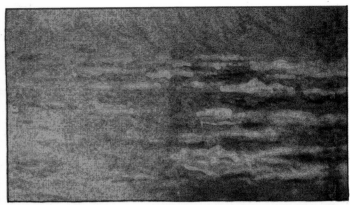

AH!

THAT DREAM AGAIN! ALWAYS THE SAME DREAM...

WHAT'S MORE, I'M DREAMING WHILE WALKING.

IF I'M DREAMING WHILE WALKING, IT'S 'CAUSE I'M DOZING WHILE WALKING.

IT'S FROM WALKING TOO MUCH.

OKAY, YOU HURRY UP NOW, HULK!

I'M FREEZING.

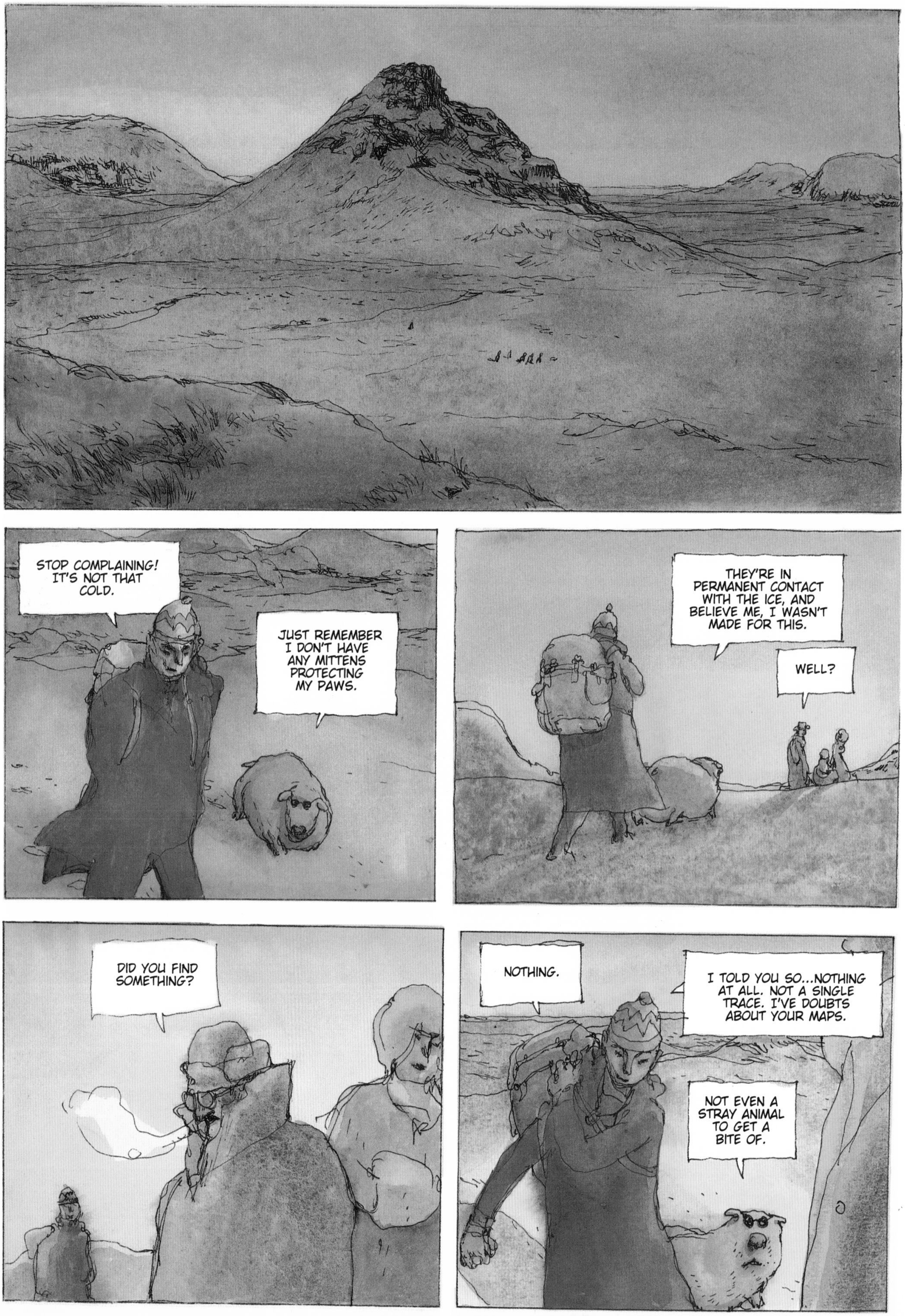
STOP COMPLAINING! IT'S NOT THAT COLD.
JUST REMEMBER I DON'T HAVE ANY MITTENS PROTECTING MY PAWS.
THEY'RE IN PERMANENT CONTACT WITH THE ICE, AND BELIEVE ME, I WASN'T MADE FOR THIS.
WELL?
DID YOU FIND SOMETHING?
NOTHING.
I TOLD YOU SO...NOTHING AT ALL. NOT A SINGLE TRACE. I'VE DOUBTS ABOUT YOUR MAPS.
NOT EVEN A STRAY ANIMAL TO GET A BITE OF.

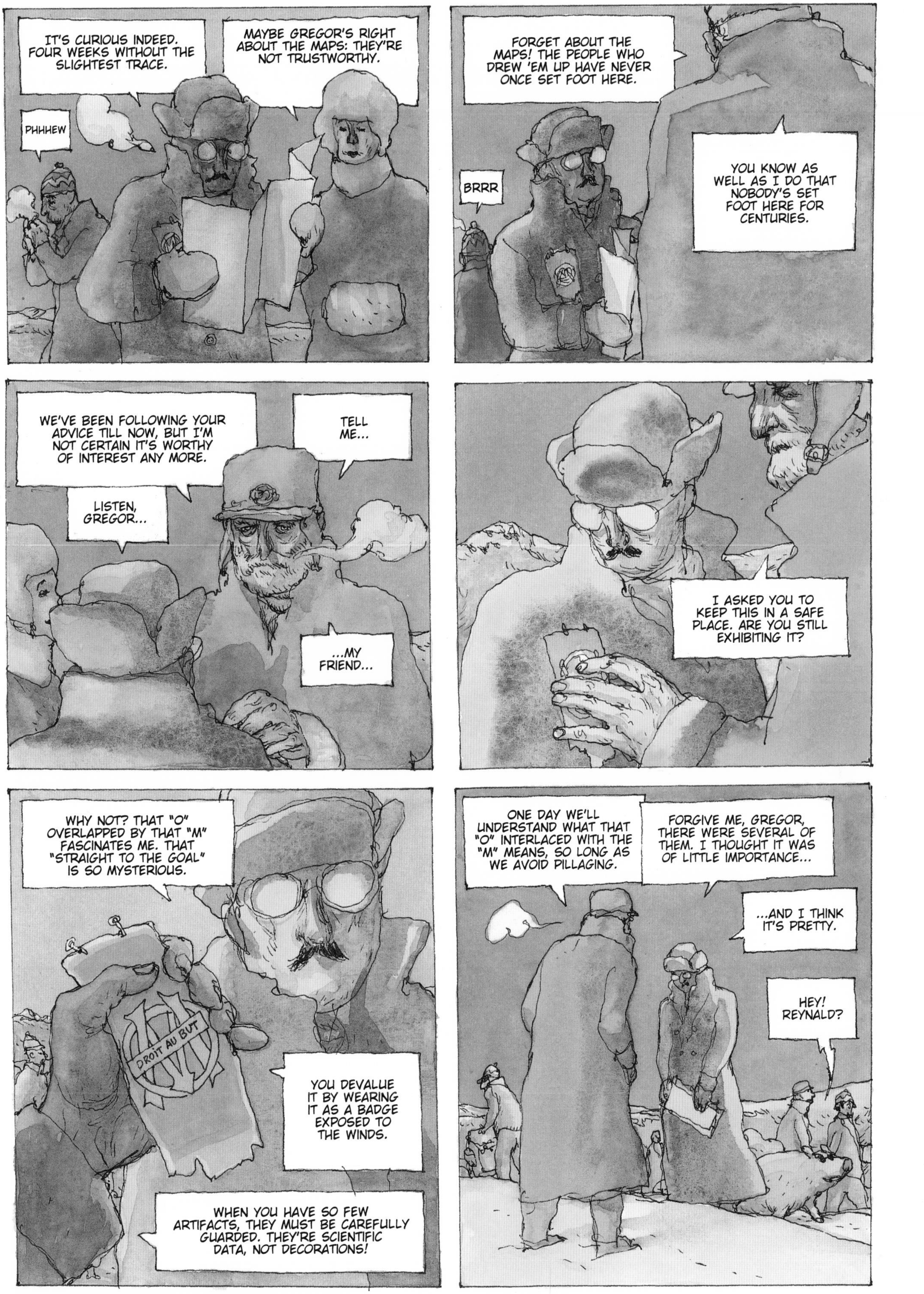
IT'S CURIOUS INDEED. FOUR WEEKS WITHOUT THE SLIGHTEST TRACE.
MAYBE GREGOR'S RIGHT ABOUT THE MAPS: THEY'RE NOT TRUSTWORTHY.
PHHHEW
FORGET ABOUT THE MAPS! THE PEOPLE WHO DREW 'EM UP HAVE NEVER ONCE SET FOOT HERE.
BRRR
YOU KNOW AS WELL AS I DO THAT NOBODY'S SET FOOT HERE FOR CENTURIES.
WE'VE BEEN FOLLOWING YOUR ADVICE TILL NOW, BUT I'M NOT CERTAIN IT'S WORTHY OF INTEREST ANY MORE.
TELL ME...
LISTEN, GREGOR...
...MY FRIEND...
I ASKED YOU TO KEEP THIS IN A SAFE PLACE. ARE YOU STILL EXHIBITING IT?
WHY NOT? THAT "O" OVERLAPPED BY THAT "M" FASCINATES ME. THAT "STRAIGHT TO THE GOAL" IS SO MYSTERIOUS.
DROIT AU BUT
YOU DEVALUE IT BY WEARING IT AS A BADGE EXPOSED TO THE WINDS.
WHEN YOU HAVE SO FEW ARTIFACTS, THEY MUST BE CAREFULLY GUARDED. THEY'RE SCIENTIFIC DATA, NOT DECORATIONS!
ONE DAY WE'LL UNDERSTAND WHAT THAT "O" INTERLACED WITH THE "M" MEANS, SO LONG AS WE AVOID PILLAGING.
FORGIVE ME, GREGOR, THERE WERE SEVERAL OF THEM. I THOUGHT IT WAS OF LITTLE IMPORTANCE...
...AND I THINK IT'S PRETTY.
HEY! REYNALD?

LOGO FOR THE SOCCER TEAM 'OLYMPIQUE DE MARSEILLE'

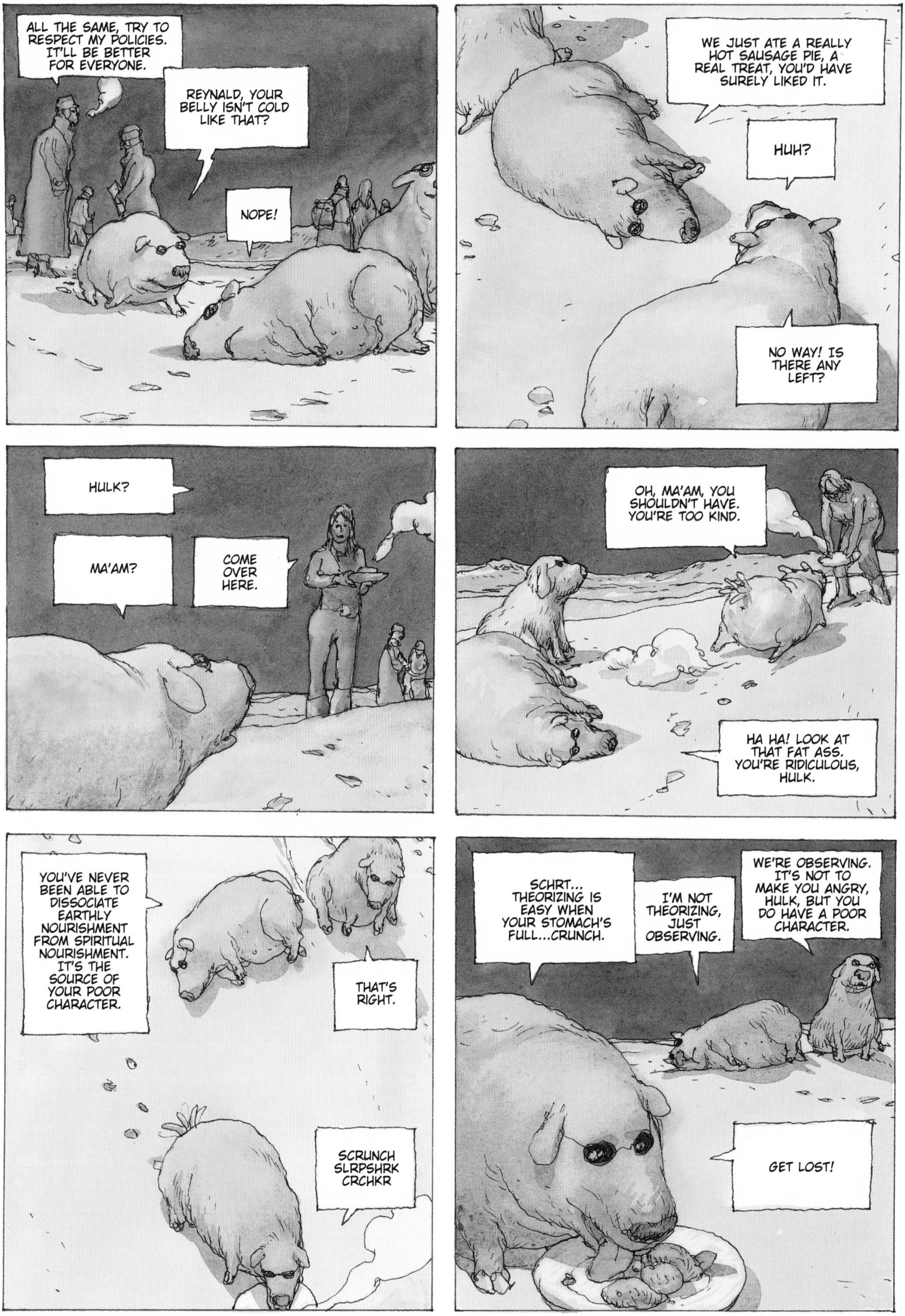
ALL THE SAME, TRY TO RESPECT MY POLICIES. IT'LL BE BETTER FOR EVERYONE.
REYNALD, YOUR BELLY ISN'T COLD LIKE THAT?
NOPE!
WE JUST ATE A REALLY HOT SAUSAGE PIE, A REAL TREAT, YOU'D HAVE SURELY LIKED IT.
HUH?
NO WAY! IS THERE ANY LEFT?
HULK?
MA'AM?
COME OVER HERE.
OH, MA'AM, YOU SHOULDN'T HAVE. YOU'RE TOO KIND.
HA HA! LOOK AT THAT FAT ASS. YOU'RE RIDICULOUS, HULK.
YOU'VE NEVER BEEN ABLE TO DISSOCIATE EARTHLY NOURISHMENT FROM SPIRITUAL NOURISHMENT. IT'S THE SOURCE OF YOUR POOR CHARACTER.
THAT'S RIGHT.
SCRUNCH SLRPSHRK CRCHKR
SCHRT... THEORIZING IS EASY WHEN YOUR STOMACH'S FULL...CRUNCH.
I'M NOT THEORIZING, JUST OBSERVING.
WE'RE OBSERVING. IT'S NOT TO MAKE YOU ANGRY, HULK, BUT YOU DO HAVE A POOR CHARACTER.
GET LOST!

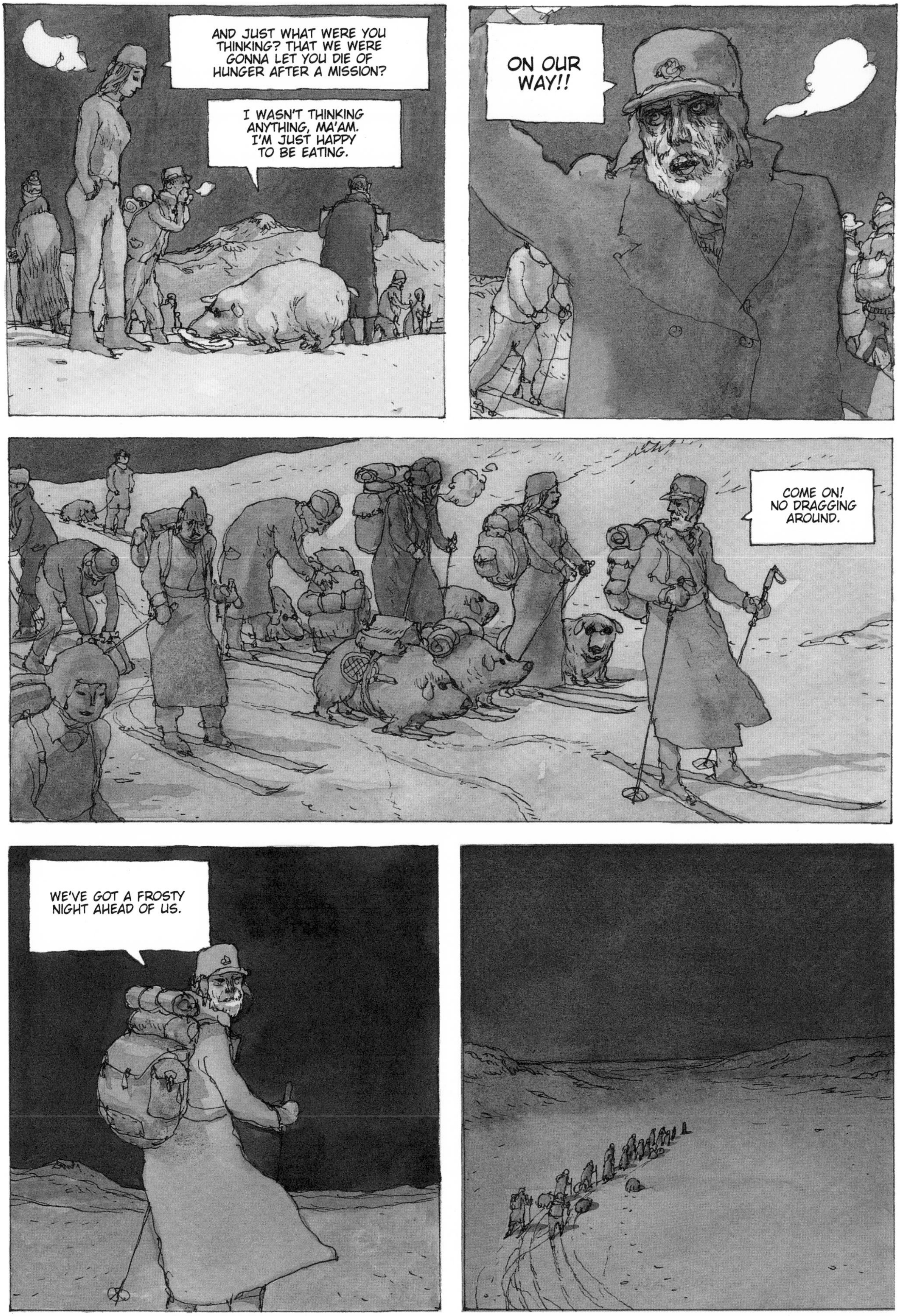
AND JUST WHAT WERE YOU THINKING? THAT WE WERE GONNA LET YOU DIE OF HUNGER AFTER A MISSION?
I WASN'T THINKING ANYTHING, MA'AM. I'M JUST HAPPY TO BE EATING.
ON OUR WAY!!
COME ON! NO DRAGGING AROUND.
WE'VE GOT A FROSTY NIGHT AHEAD OF US.

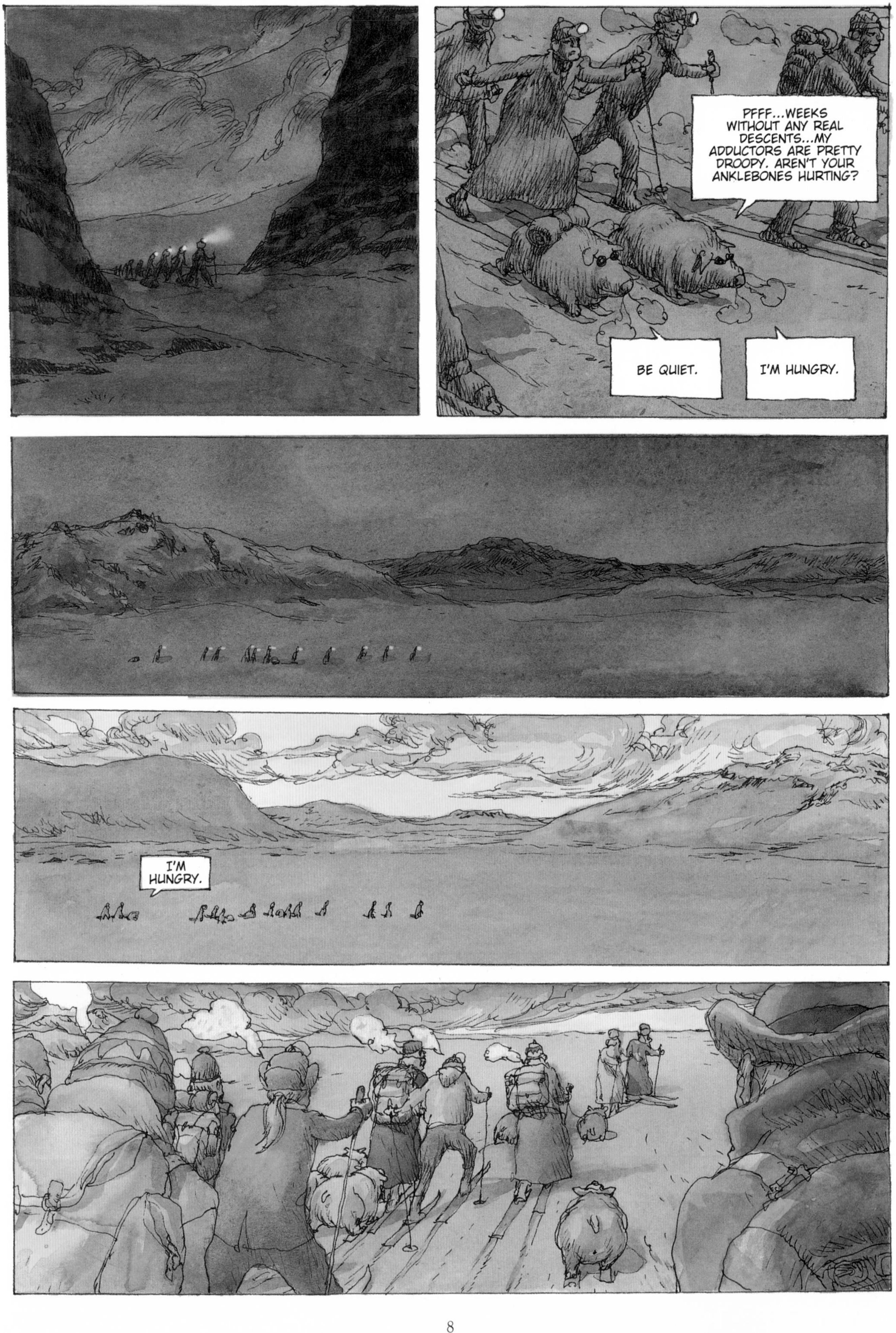
PFFF...WEEKS WITHOUT ANY REAL DESCENTS...MY ADDUCTORS ARE PRETTY DROOPY. AREN'T YOUR ANKLEBONES HURTING?
BE QUIET.
I'M HUNGRY.
I'M HUNGRY.

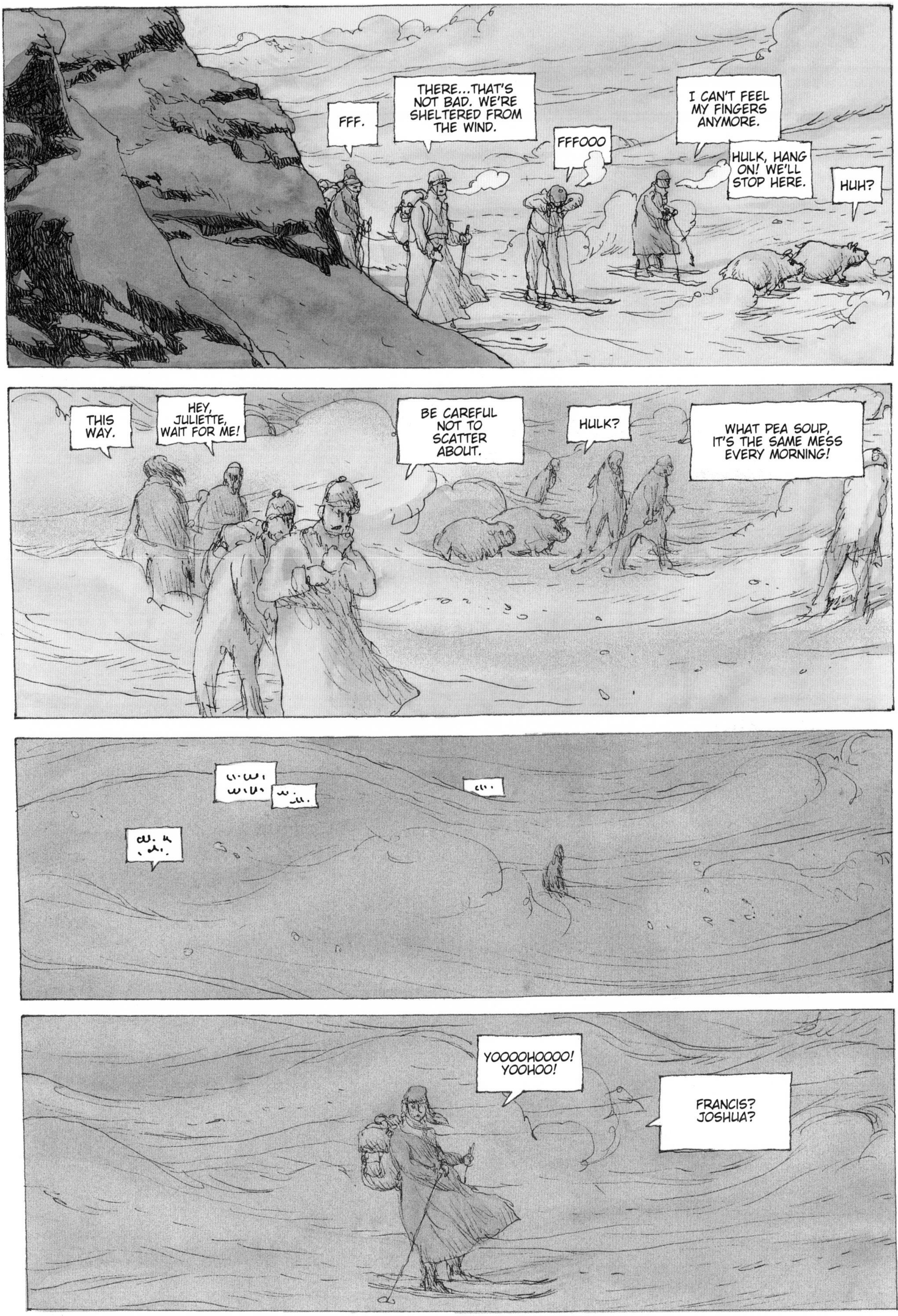
FFF.
THERE...THAT'S NOT BAD. WE'RE SHELTERED FROM THE WIND.
FFFOOO
I CAN'T FEEL MY FINGERS ANYMORE.
HULK, HANG ON! WE'LL STOP HERE.
HUH?
THIS WAY.
HEY, JULIETTE, WAIT FOR ME!
BE CAREFUL NOT TO SCATTER ABOUT.
HULK?
WHAT PEA SOUP, IT'S THE SAME MESS EVERY MORNING!
YOOOOHOOOO! YOOHOO!
FRANCIS? JOSHUA?

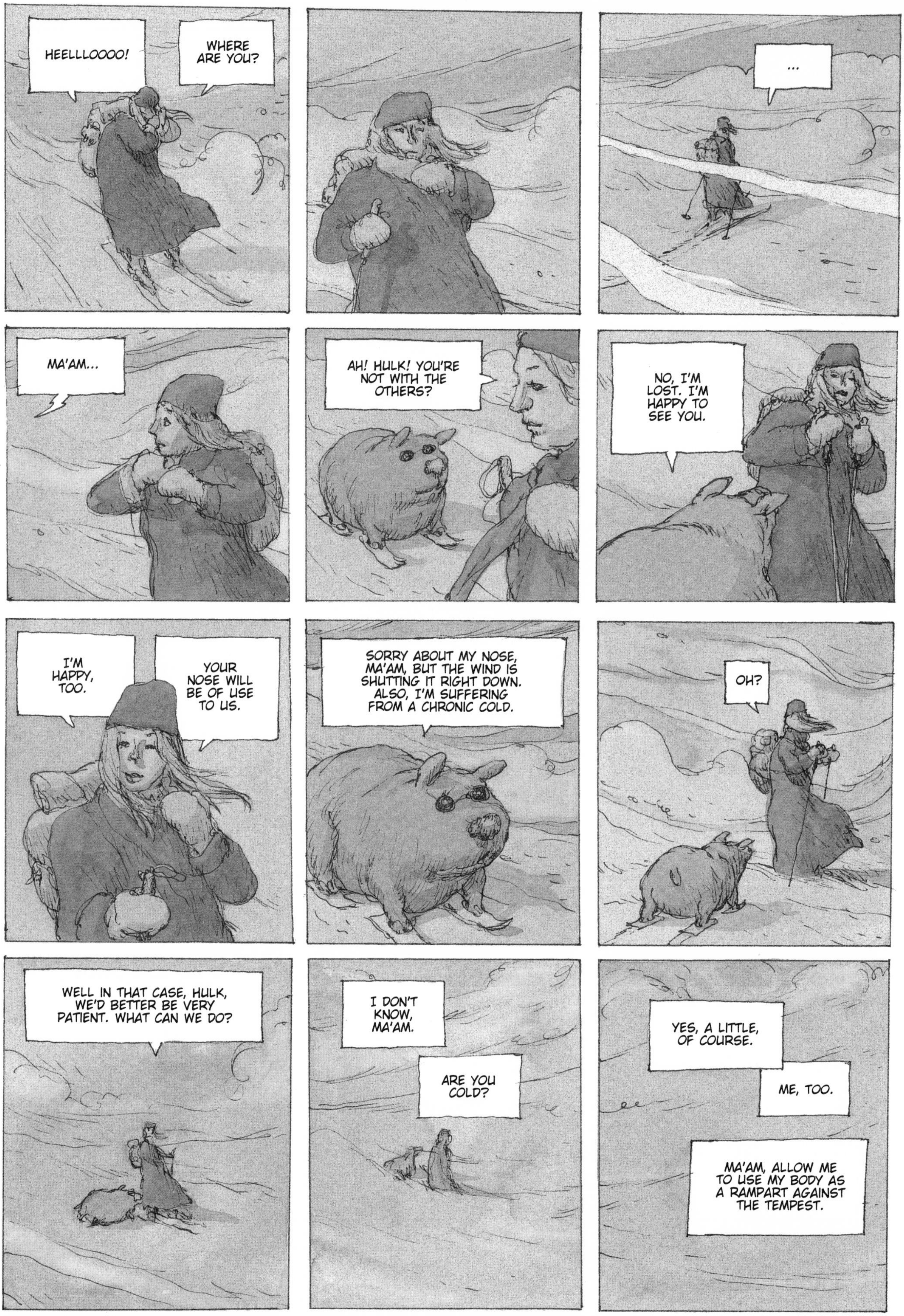
HEELLLOOOO!
WHERE ARE YOU?
...
MA'AM...
AH! HULK! YOU'RE NOT WITH THE OTHERS?
NO, I'M LOST. I'M HAPPY TO SEE YOU.
I'M HAPPY, TOO.
YOUR NOSE WILL BE OF USE TO US.
SORRY ABOUT MY NOSE, MA'AM, BUT THE WIND IS SHUTTING IT RIGHT DOWN. ALSO, I'M SUFFERING FROM A CHRONIC COLD.
OH?
WELL IN THAT CASE, HULK, WE'D BETTER BE VERY PATIENT. WHAT CAN WE DO?
I DON'T KNOW, MA'AM.
ARE YOU COLD?
YES, A LITTLE, OF COURSE.
ME, TOO.
MA'AM, ALLOW ME TO USE MY BODY AS A RAMPART AGAINST THE TEMPEST.

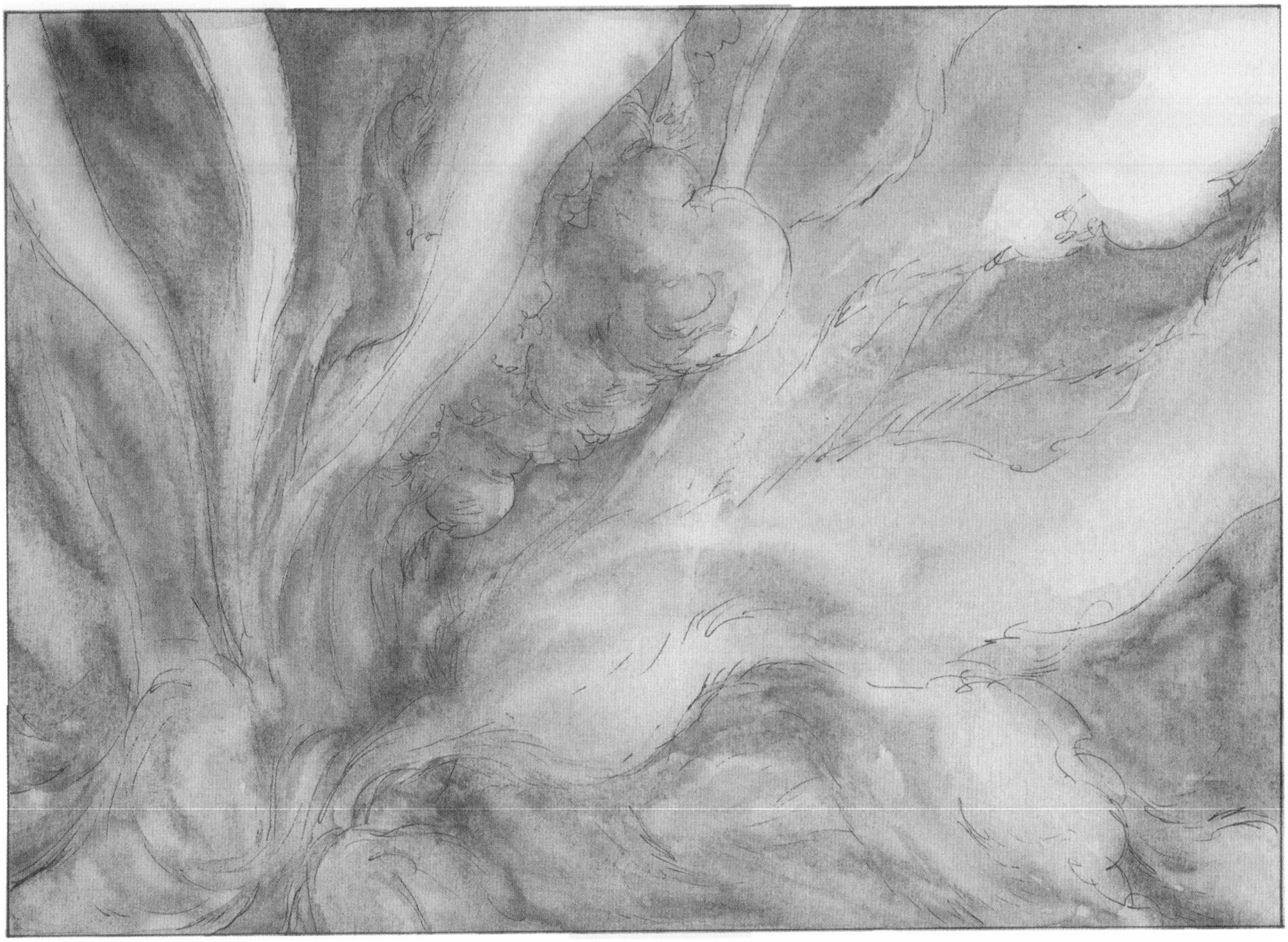

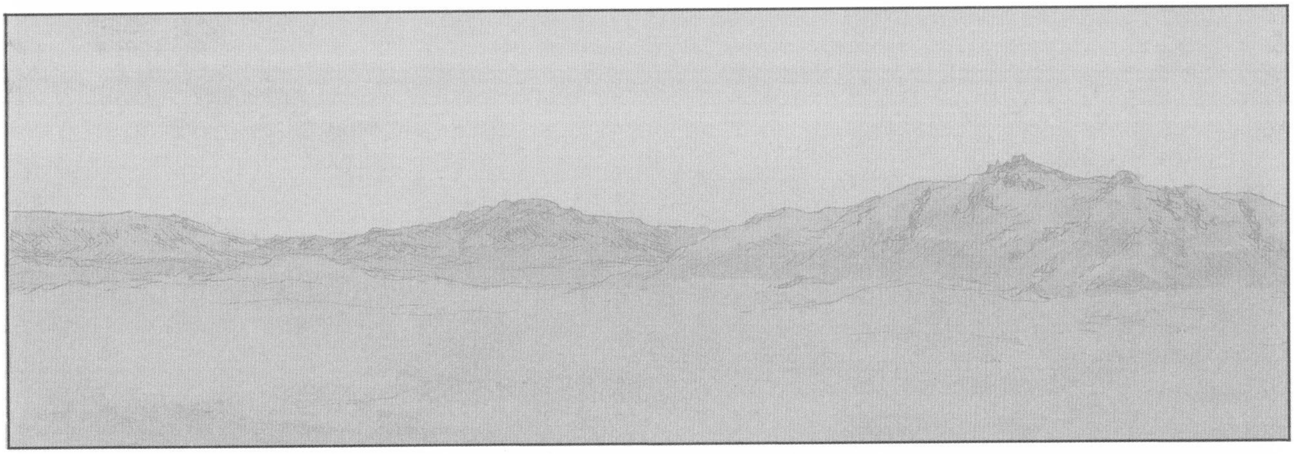

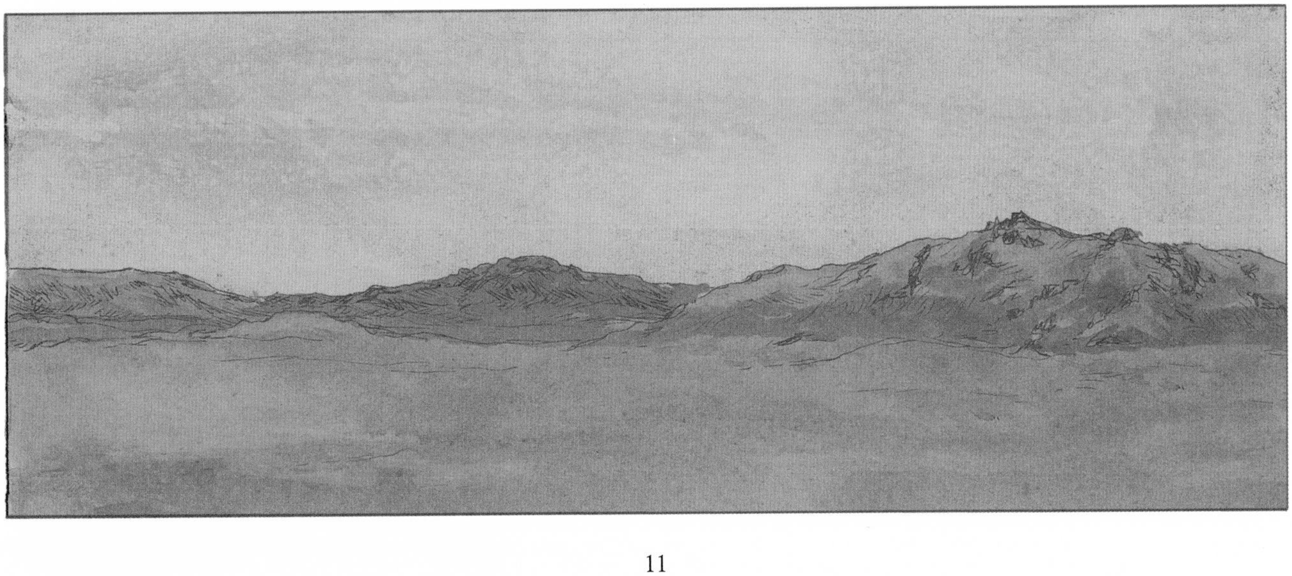

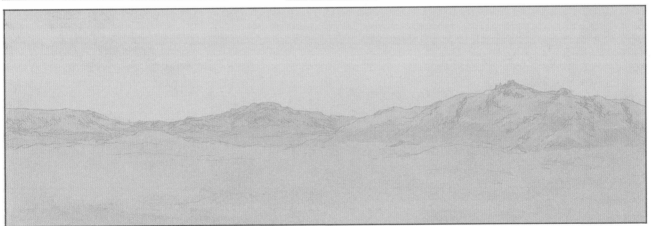

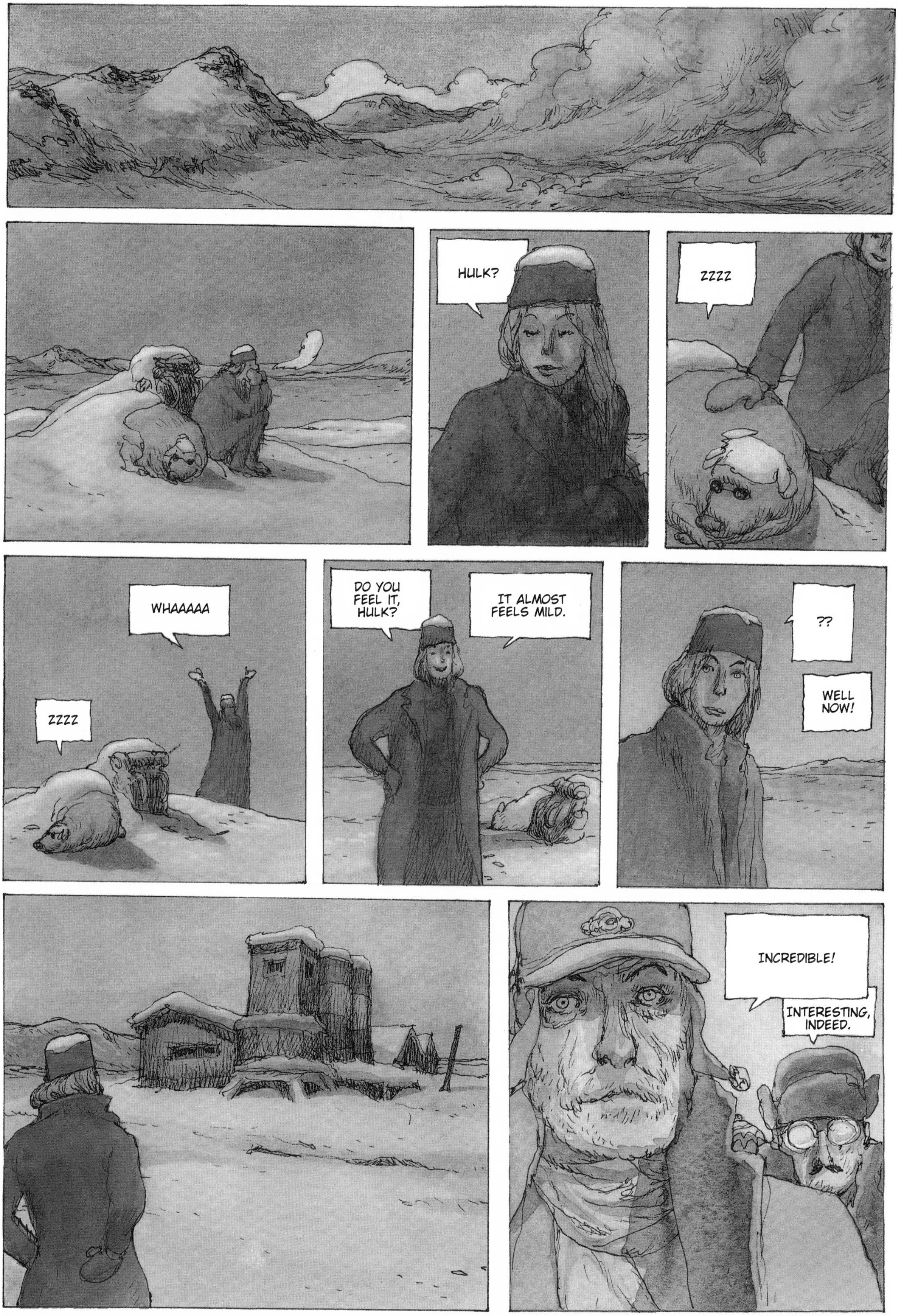
HULK?
ZZZZ
WHAAAAA
ZZZZ
DO YOU FEEL IT, HULK?
IT ALMOST FEELS MILD.
??
WELL NOW!
INCREDIBLE!
INTERESTING, INDEED.

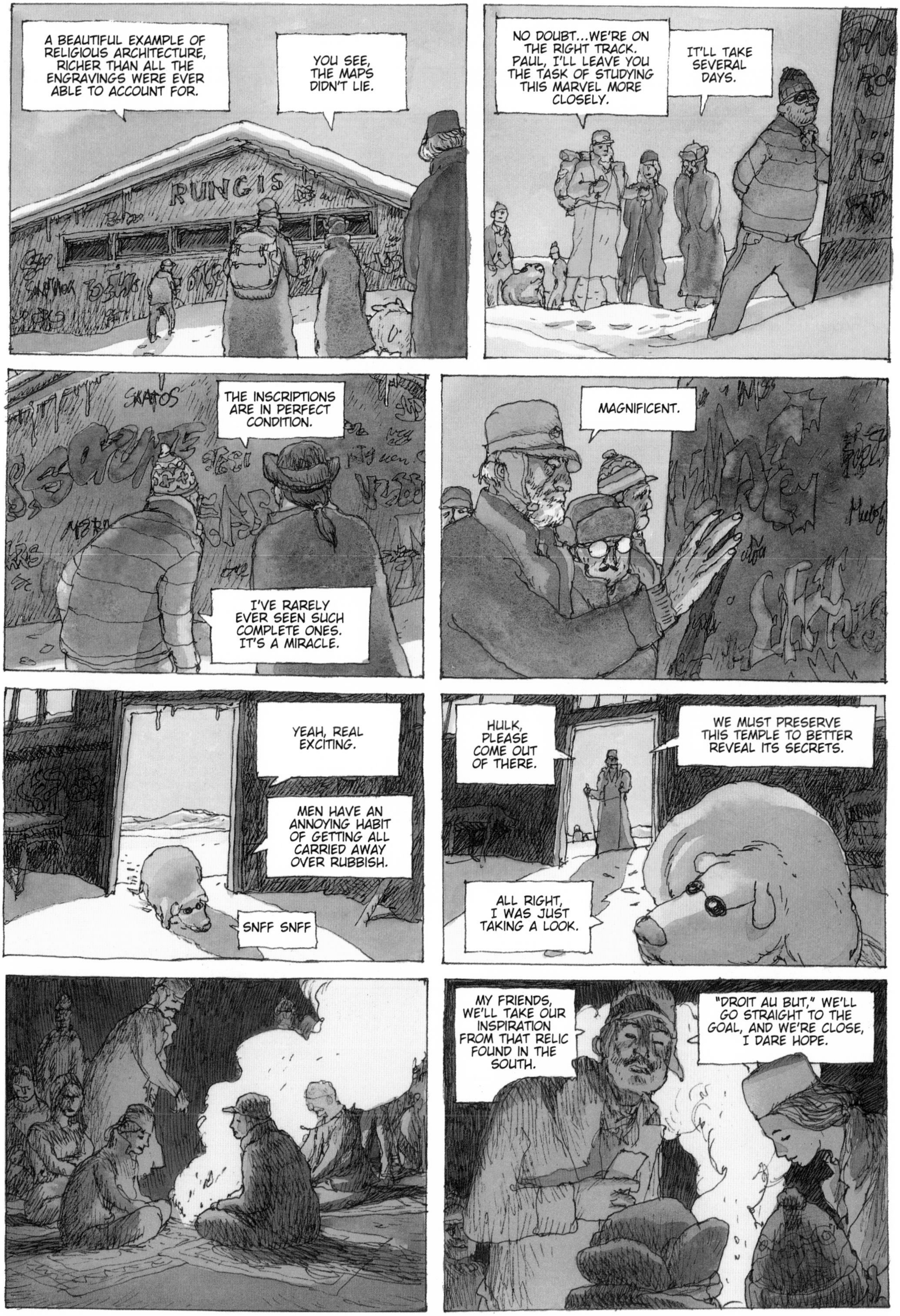
A BEAUTIFUL EXAMPLE OF RELIGIOUS ARCHITECTURE, RICHER THAN ALL THE ENGRAVINGS WERE EVER ABLE TO ACCOUNT FOR.
YOU SEE, THE MAPS DIDN'T LIE.
RUNGIS
NO DOUBT...WE'RE ON THE RIGHT TRACK. PAUL, I'LL LEAVE YOU THE TASK OF STUDYING THIS MARVEL MORE CLOSELY.
IT'LL TAKE SEVERAL DAYS.
THE INSCRIPTIONS ARE IN PERFECT CONDITION.
I'VE RARELY EVER SEEN SUCH COMPLETE ONES. IT'S A MIRACLE.
MAGNIFICENT.
YEAH, REAL EXCITING.
MEN HAVE AN ANNOYING HABIT OF GETTING ALL CARRIED AWAY OVER RUBBISH.
SNFF SNFF
HULK, PLEASE COME OUT OF THERE.
WE MUST PRESERVE THIS TEMPLE TO BETTER REVEAL ITS SECRETS.
ALL RIGHT, I WAS JUST TAKING A LOOK.
MY FRIENDS, WE'LL TAKE OUR INSPIRATION FROM THAT RELIC FOUND IN THE SOUTH.
"DROIT AU BUT," WE'LL GO STRAIGHT TO THE GOAL, AND WE'RE CLOSE, I DARE HOPE.

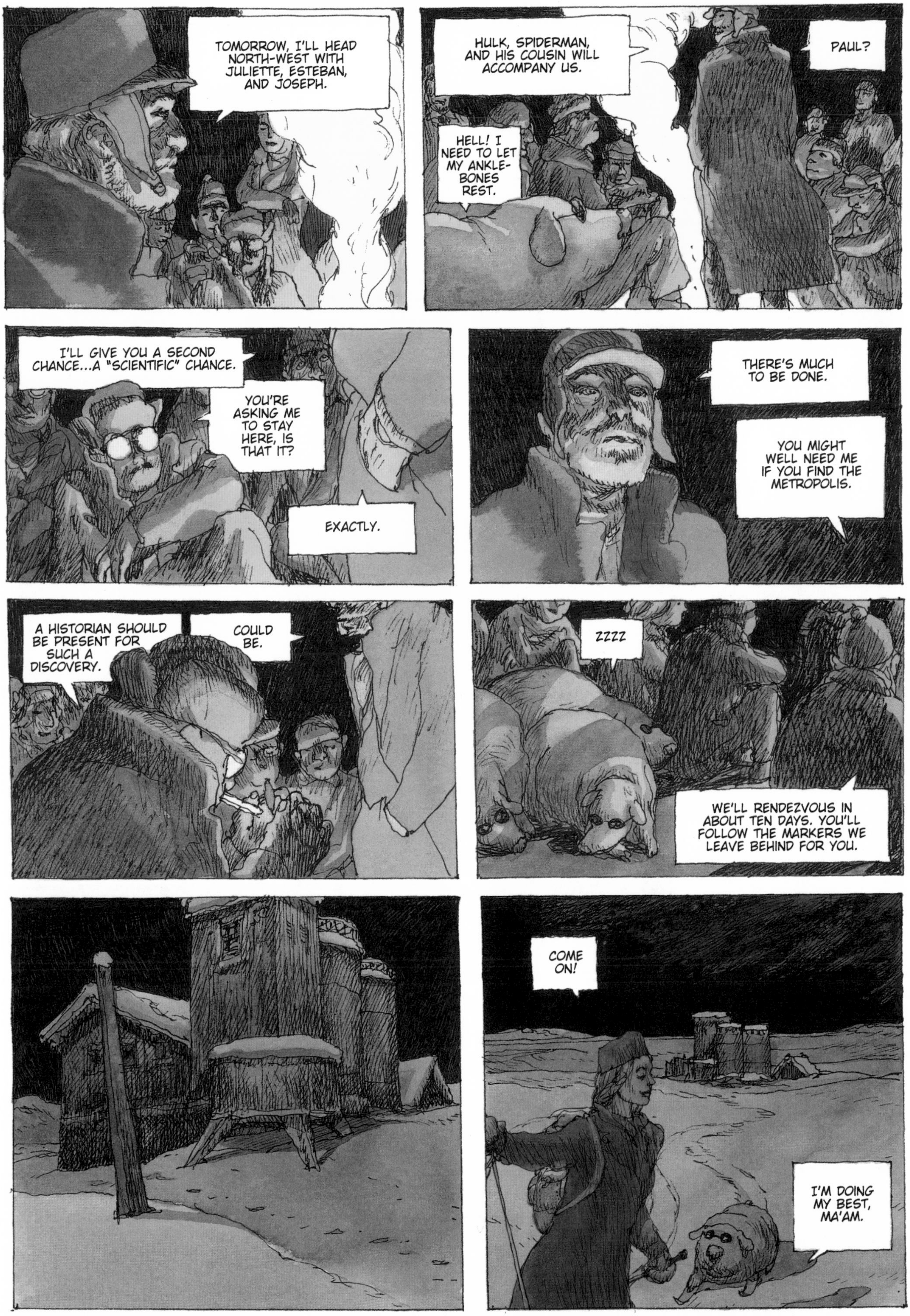
TOMORROW, I'LL HEAD NORTH-WEST WITH JULIETTE, ESTEBAN, AND JOSEPH.
HULK, SPIDERMAN, AND HIS COUSIN WILL ACCOMPANY US.
HELL! I NEED TO LET MY ANKLE-BONES REST.
PAUL?
I'LL GIVE YOU A SECOND CHANCE...A "SCIENTIFIC" CHANCE.
YOU'RE ASKING ME TO STAY HERE, IS THAT IT?
EXACTLY.
THERE'S MUCH TO BE DONE.
YOU MIGHT WELL NEED ME IF YOU FIND THE METROPOLIS.
A HISTORIAN SHOULD BE PRESENT FOR SUCH A DISCOVERY.
COULD BE.
ZZZZ
WE'LL RENDEZVOUS IN ABOUT TEN DAYS. YOU'LL FOLLOW THE MARKERS WE LEAVE BEHIND FOR YOU.
COME ON!
I'M DOING MY BEST, MA'AM.

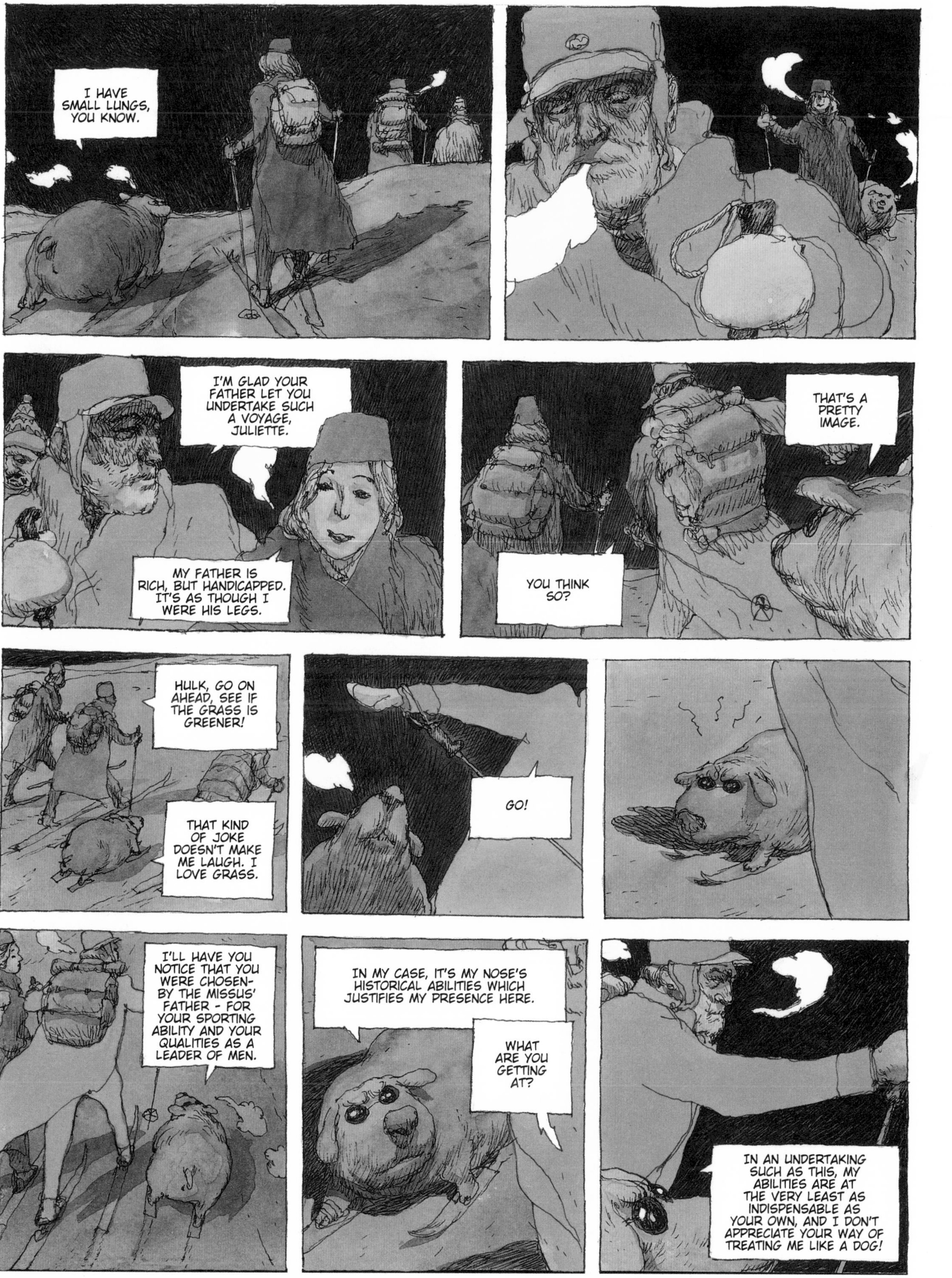
I HAVE SMALL LUNGS, YOU KNOW.
I'M GLAD YOUR FATHER LET YOU UNDERTAKE SUCH A VOYAGE, JULIETTE.
MY FATHER IS RICH, BUT HANDICAPPED. IT'S AS THOUGH I WERE HIS LEGS.
THAT'S A PRETTY IMAGE.
YOU THINK SO?
HULK, GO ON AHEAD, SEE IF THE GRASS IS GREENER!
THAT KIND OF JOKE DOESN'T MAKE ME LAUGH. I LOVE GRASS.
GO!
I'LL HAVE YOU NOTICE THAT YOU WERE CHOSEN- BY THE MISSUS' FATHER - FOR YOUR SPORTING ABILITY AND YOUR QUALITIES AS A LEADER OF MEN.
IN MY CASE, IT'S MY NOSE'S HISTORICAL ABILITIES WHICH JUSTIFIES MY PRESENCE HERE.
WHAT ARE YOU GETTING AT?
IN AN UNDERTAKING SUCH AS THIS, MY ABILITIES ARE AT THE VERY LEAST AS INDISPENSABLE AS YOUR OWN, AND I DON'T APPRECIATE YOUR WAY OF TREATING ME LIKE A DOG!

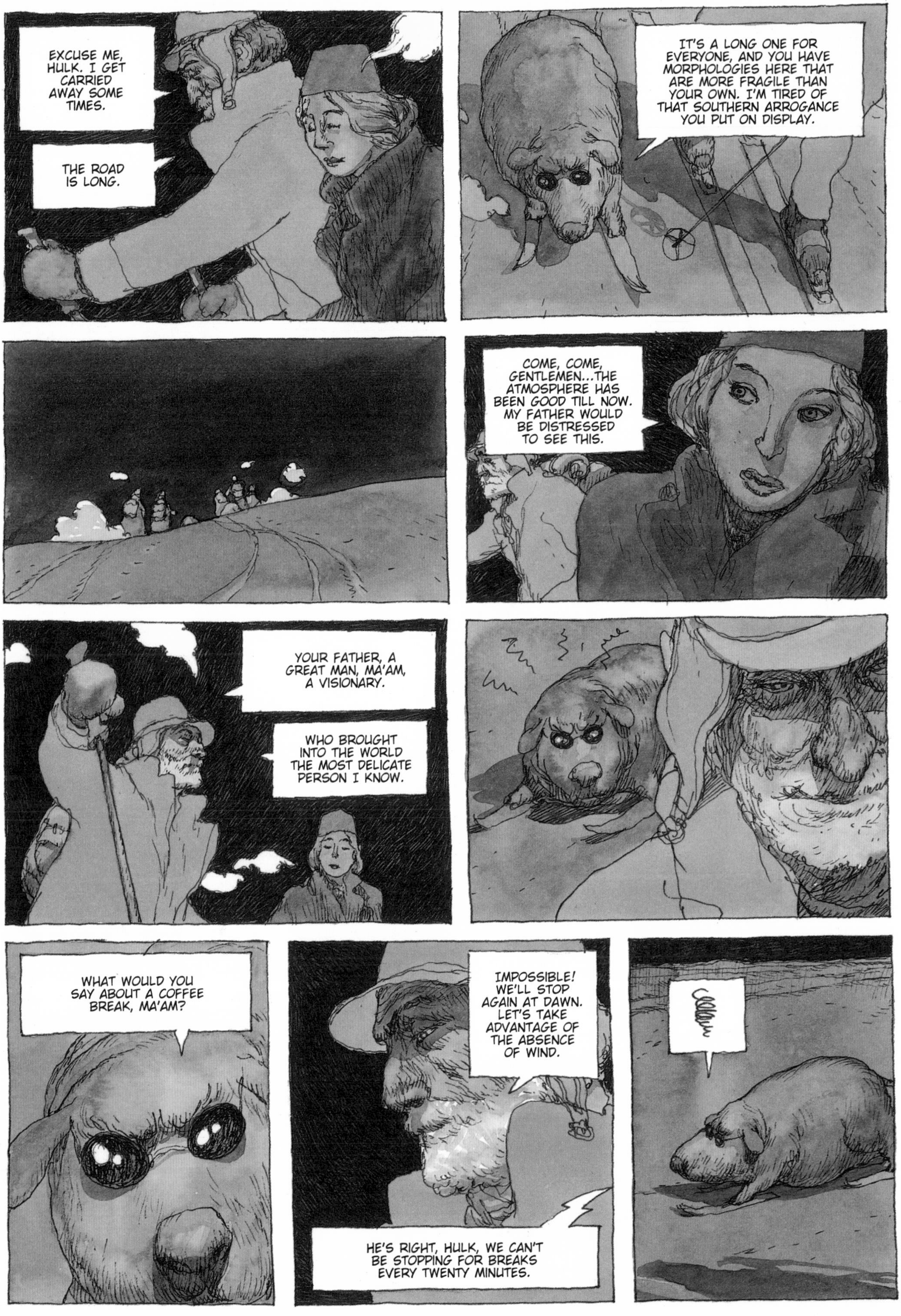
EXCUSE ME, HULK. I GET CARRIED AWAY SOME TIMES.
THE ROAD IS LONG.
IT'S A LONG ONE FOR EVERYONE, AND YOU HAVE MORPHOLOGIES HERE THAT ARE MORE FRAGILE THAN YOUR OWN. I'M TIRED OF THAT SOUTHERN ARROGANCE YOU PUT ON DISPLAY.
COME, COME, GENTLEMEN...THE ATMOSPHERE HAS BEEN GOOD TILL NOW. MY FATHER WOULD BE DISTRESSED TO SEE THIS.
YOUR FATHER, A GREAT MAN, MA'AM, A VISIONARY.
WHO BROUGHT INTO THE WORLD THE MOST DELICATE PERSON I KNOW.
WHAT WOULD YOU SAY ABOUT A COFFEE BREAK, MA'AM?
IMPOSSIBLE! WE'LL STOP AGAIN AT DAWN. LET'S TAKE ADVANTAGE OF THE ABSENCE OF WIND.
HE'S RIGHT, HULK, WE CAN'T BE STOPPING FOR BREAKS EVERY TWENTY MINUTES.

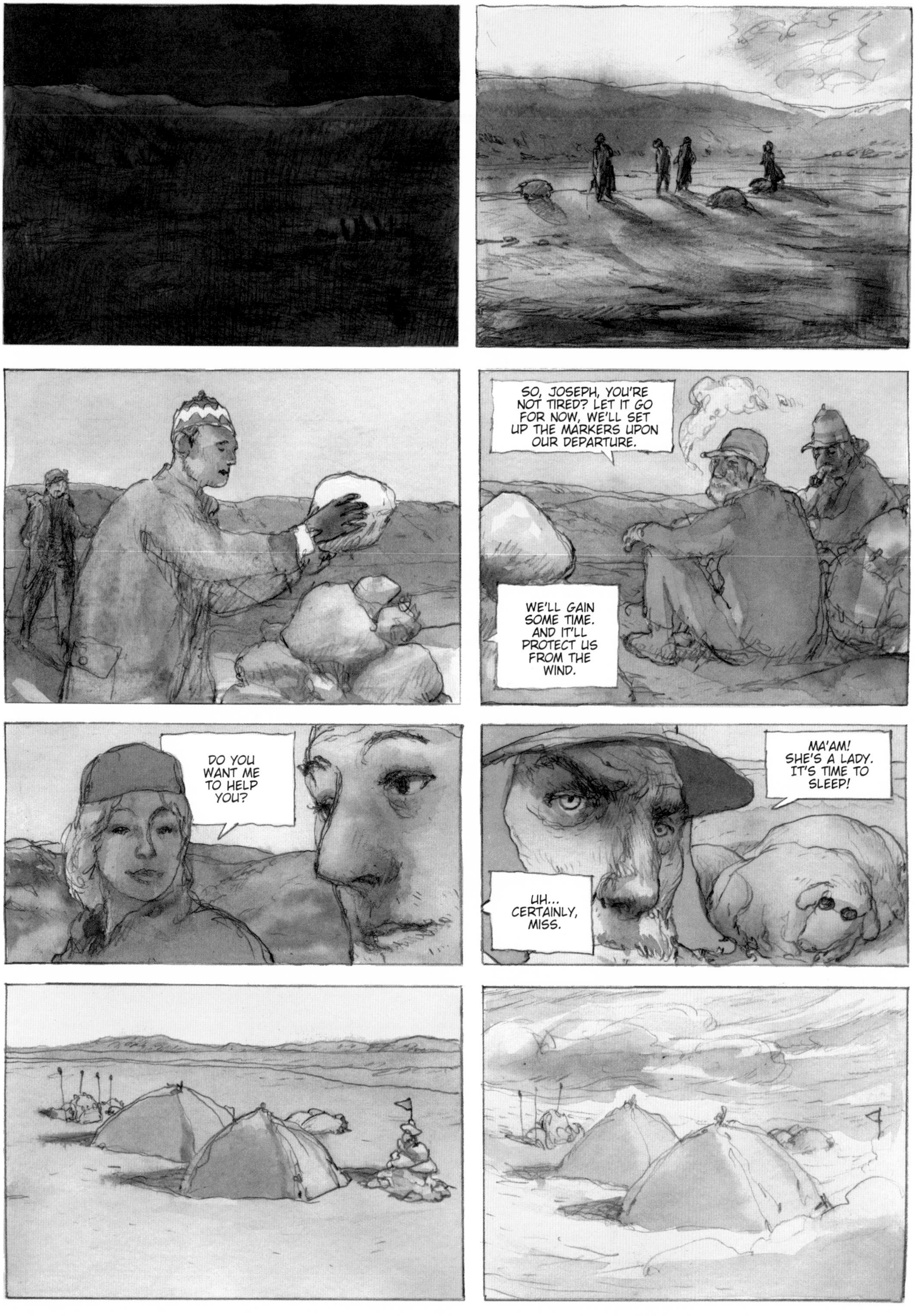
SO, JOSEPH, YOU'RE NOT TIRED? LET IT GO FOR NOW, WE'LL SET UP THE MARKERS UPON OUR DEPARTURE.
WE'LL GAIN SOME TIME. AND IT'LL PROTECT US FROM THE WIND.
DO YOU WANT ME TO HELP YOU?
MA'AM! SHE'S A LADY. IT'S TIME TO SLEEP!
UH... CERTAINLY, MISS.

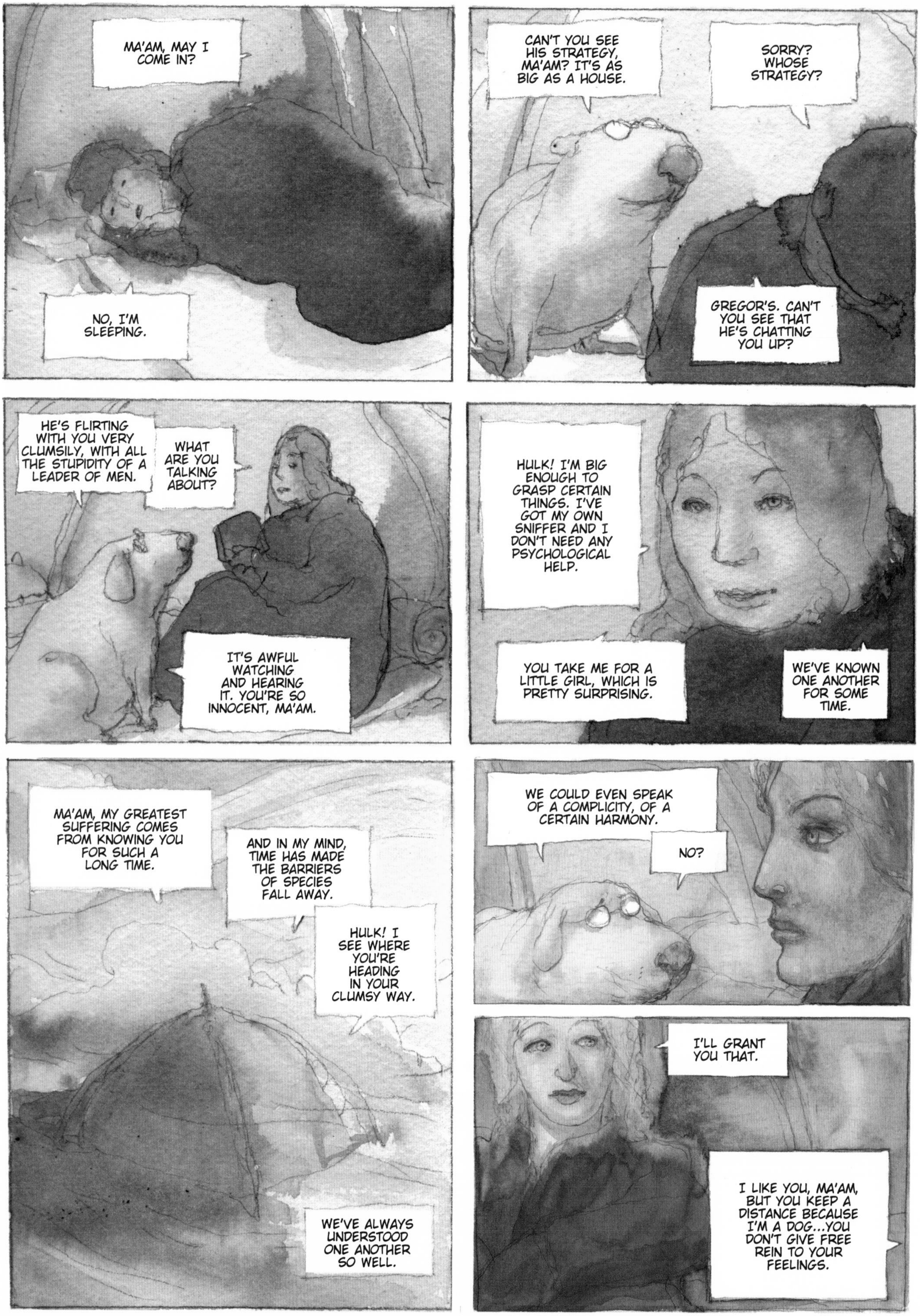
MA'AM, MAY I COME IN?
NO, I'M SLEEPING.
CAN'T YOU SEE HIS STRATEGY, MA'AM? IT'S AS BIG AS A HOUSE.
SORRY? WHOSE STRATEGY?
GREGOR'S. CAN'T YOU SEE THAT HE'S CHATTING YOU UP?
HE'S FLIRTING WITH YOU VERY CLUMSILY, WITH ALL THE STUPIDITY OF A LEADER OF MEN.
WHAT ARE YOU TALKING ABOUT?
IT'S AWFUL WATCHING AND HEARING IT. YOU'RE SO INNOCENT, MA'AM.
HULK! I'M BIG ENOUGH TO GRASP CERTAIN THINGS. I'VE GOT MY OWN SNIFFER AND I DON'T NEED ANY PSYCHOLOGICAL HELP.
YOU TAKE ME FOR A LITTLE GIRL, WHICH IS PRETTY SURPRISING.
WE'VE KNOWN ONE ANOTHER FOR SOME TIME.
MA'AM, MY GREATEST SUFFERING COMES FROM KNOWING YOU FOR SUCH A LONG TIME.
AND IN MY MIND, TIME HAS MADE THE BARRIERS OF SPECIES FALL AWAY.
HULK! I SEE WHERE YOU'RE HEADING IN YOUR CLUMSY WAY.
WE'VE ALWAYS UNDERSTOOD ONE ANOTHER SO WELL.
WE COULD EVEN SPEAK OF A COMPLICITY, OF A CERTAIN HARMONY.
NO?
I'LL GRANT YOU THAT.
I LIKE YOU, MA'AM, BUT YOU KEEP A DISTANCE BECAUSE I'M A DOG...YOU DON'T GIVE FREE REIN TO YOUR FEELINGS.

COME ON, HULK! OUR COMPLICITY IS BASED PRECISELY ON OUR FRIENDSHIP. YOU KNOW IT FULL WELL. YOU'RE THE ONE WHO'S PLAYING AT FALSE INNOCENCE.
I DON'T UNDERSTAND YOUR ATTITUDE ALL THAT WELL. WHAT YOU'RE WANTING TO CHANGE WOULDN'T COME TO ANYTHING.
OF COURSE, OF COURSE...
BUT ALL IT WOULD TAKE IS FOR MY CORPOREAL SHELL TO BE DIFFERENT FOR YOU TO LOVE ME COMPLETELY. THE IMAGE I SEND BACK TO YOU ISN'T GRATIFYING TO YOU.
. LIKE IN A DISTORTING MIRROR.
I'M SLEEPY.
ARE YOU ASLEEP?
YES.
IMAGINE ME WITH A HANDSOME MUG AND BLUE EYES.
HUH?

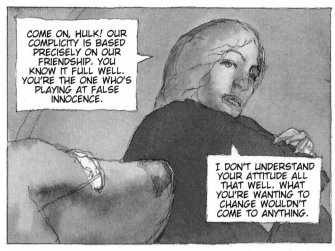

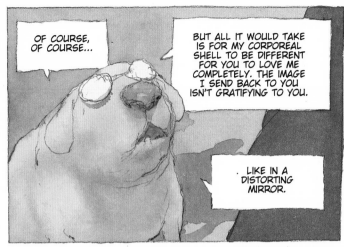

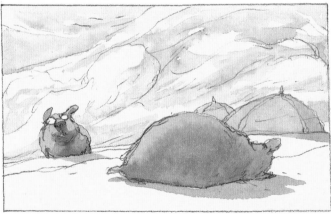

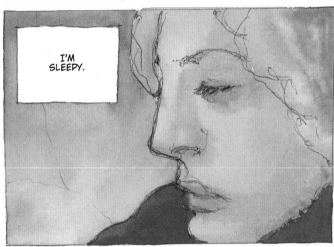

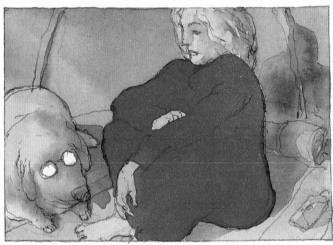

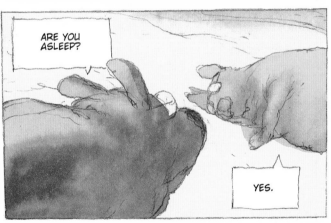

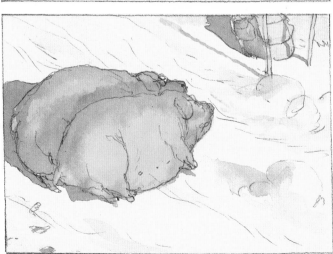

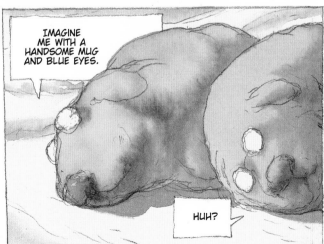

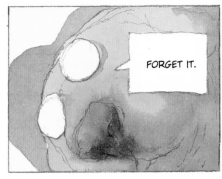

FORGET IT.

IT'S CLEARING UP. WE'LL BE ABLE TO GET GOING.

AND HULK?

HE MUST HAVE GONE FOR A WALK. YOU KNOW HIM.

STILL, I'M WORRIED.

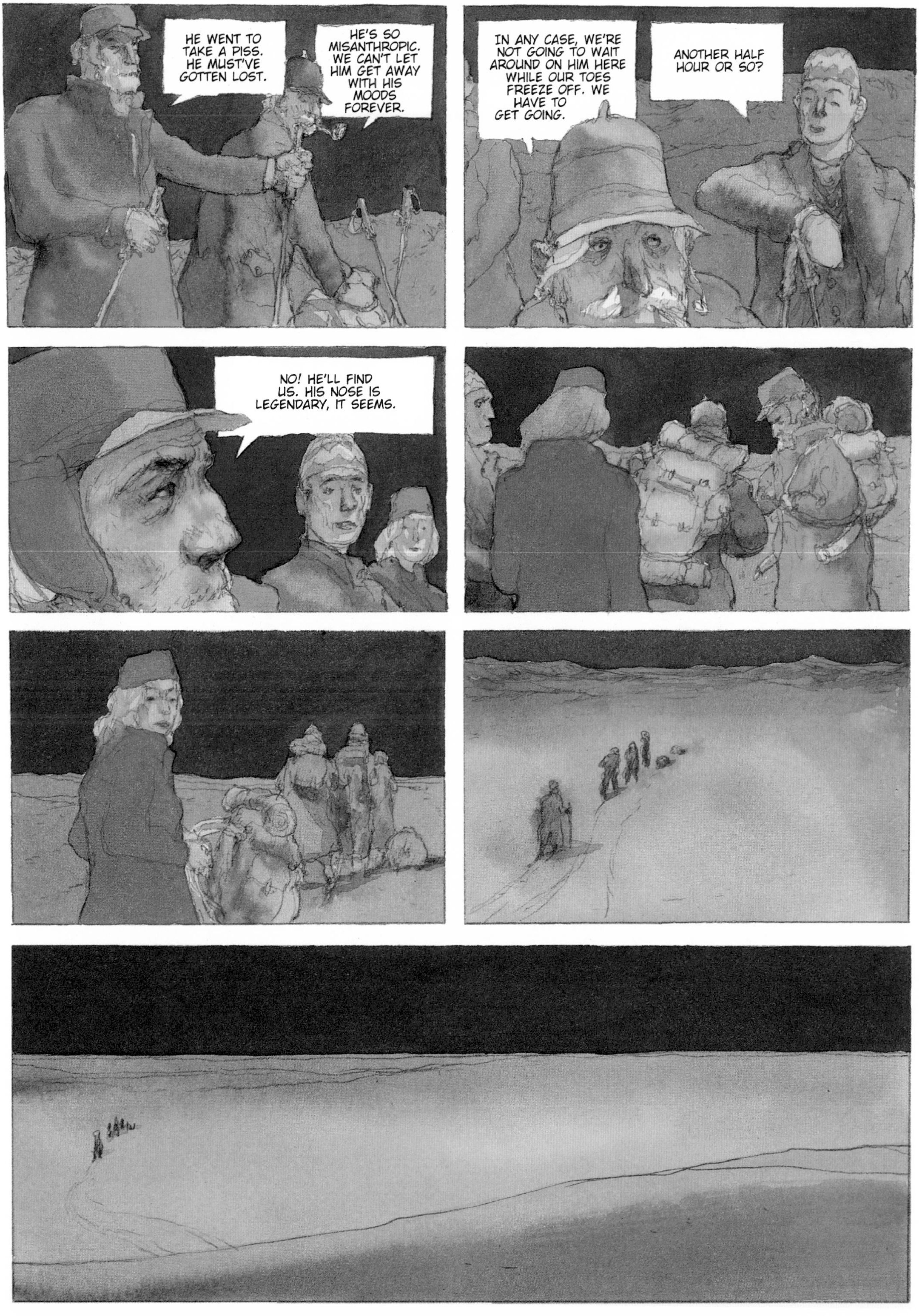
HE WENT TO TAKE A PISS. HE MUST'VE GOTTEN LOST.
HE'S SO MISANTHROPIC. WE CAN'T LET HIM GET AWAY WITH HIS MOODS FOREVER.
IN ANY CASE, WE'RE NOT GOING TO WAIT AROUND ON HIM HERE WHILE OUR TOES FREEZE OFF. WE HAVE TO GET GOING.
ANOTHER HALF HOUR OR SO?
NO! HE'LL FIND US. HIS NOSE IS LEGENDARY, IT SEEMS.

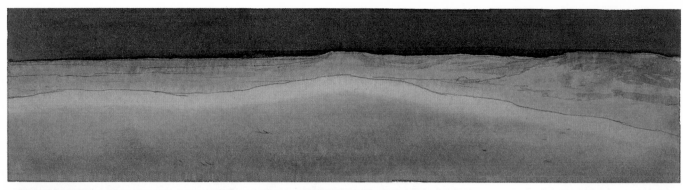

ZZZZZ RRRZZZ

RZZ... HM!

NIGHT ALREADY?

FLAP FLAP FLAP!

SNFF SNFF

THE SNOW COVERED OVER MY TRACKS.

SNFF SNFF... STILL THIS BLASTED COLD.

SNFF.

I MUST BE ALLERGIC TO SOMETHING, SNFF SNFF.

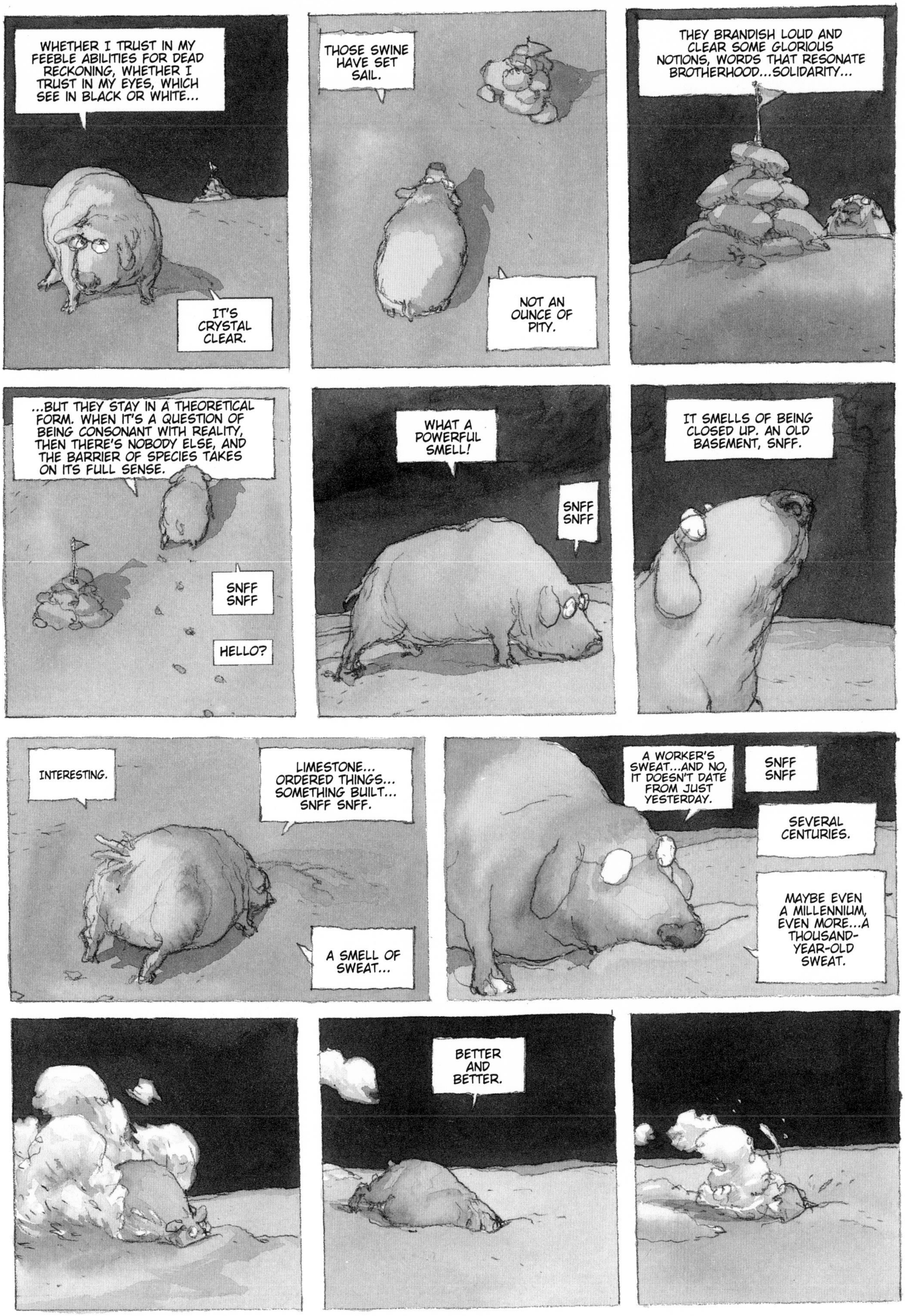
WHETHER I TRUST IN MY FEEBLE ABILITIES FOR DEAD RECKONING, WHETHER I TRUST IN MY EYES, WHICH SEE IN BLACK OR WHITE...
IT'S CRYSTAL CLEAR.
THOSE SWINE HAVE SET SAIL.
NOT AN OUNCE OF PITY.
THEY BRANDISH LOUD AND CLEAR SOME GLORIOUS NOTIONS, WORDS THAT RESONATE BROTHERHOOD...SOLIDARITY...
...BUT THEY STAY IN A THEORETICAL FORM. WHEN IT'S A QUESTION OF BEING CONSONANT WITH REALITY, THEN THERE'S NOBODY ELSE, AND THE BARRIER OF SPECIES TAKES ON ITS FULL SENSE.
SNFF SNFF
HELLO?
WHAT A POWERFUL SMELL!
SNFF SNFF
IT SMELLS OF BEING CLOSED UP. AN OLD BASEMENT, SNFF.
INTERESTING.
LIMESTONE... ORDERED THINGS... SOMETHING BUILT... SNFF SNFF.
A SMELL OF SWEAT...
A WORKER'S SWEAT...AND NO, IT DOESN'T DATE FROM JUST YESTERDAY.
SNFF SNFF
SEVERAL CENTURIES.
MAYBE EVEN A MILLENNIUM, EVEN MORE...A THOUSAND-YEAR-OLD SWEAT.
BETTER AND BETTER.

A DRAINFIELD....EVEN OLDER...A DRAIN THAT ALLOWED CONSTRUCTION.

THE EXCITEMENT'S CLEARING UP MY SNOUT!

SNFF SNFF SNFF! THERE'S STUFF HERE. IT'S AN INCREDIBLE TRAIL. IF THE OTHERS KNEW ABOUT IT, THEY'D BE WEEPING!

SNFF SNFF. A RIVER...A FROZEN RIVER.

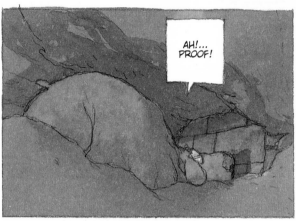

AH!... PROOF!

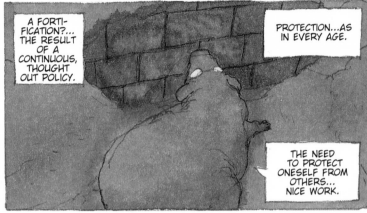

A FORTI- FICATION?... THE RESULT OF A CONTINUOUS, THOUGHT OUT POLICY.

PROTECTION...AS IN EVERY AGE.

THE NEED TO PROTECT ONESELF FROM OTHERS... NICE WORK.

OOPS!

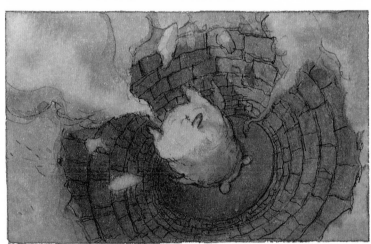

OOOOF!

OUCH!

?!

I'M RICH.

COINS, PIECES OF GOLD...NO, IT'S NOT MADE OF GOLD.

24

...A CRUDE ALLOY... TWO EUROS, SNFF SNFF, TWO YEARS, TWO THOUSAND.... MAYBE THE YEAR TWO THOUSAND.

A ROUND NUMBER FOR A CATASTROPHE.

EURO...EURO, A PRINCESS'S NAME... UNLESS IT'S A MAP... YES, IT LOOKS LIKE A MAP...SNFF SNFF.

SNFF SNFF.

THE MAP OF THE LOST CONTINENT, OF THE FROZEN CONTINENT. THAT'S IT.

EURO: THE FROZEN CONTINENT, NOW WE KNOW ITS NAME.

ITS NAME AND THE CONTOURS OF ITS SHAPE... SNFF SNFF.

SNFF SNFF

SNFF SNFF

THE ANCIENT PRESENCE OF WATER.

A WELL, NO DOUBT, BEFORE BECOMING A MAP LIBRARY.

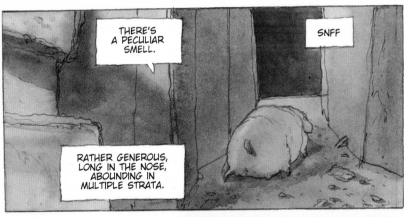

THERE'S A PECULIAR SMELL.

SNFF

RATHER GENEROUS, LONG IN THE NOSE, ABOUNDING IN MULTIPLE STRATA.

?

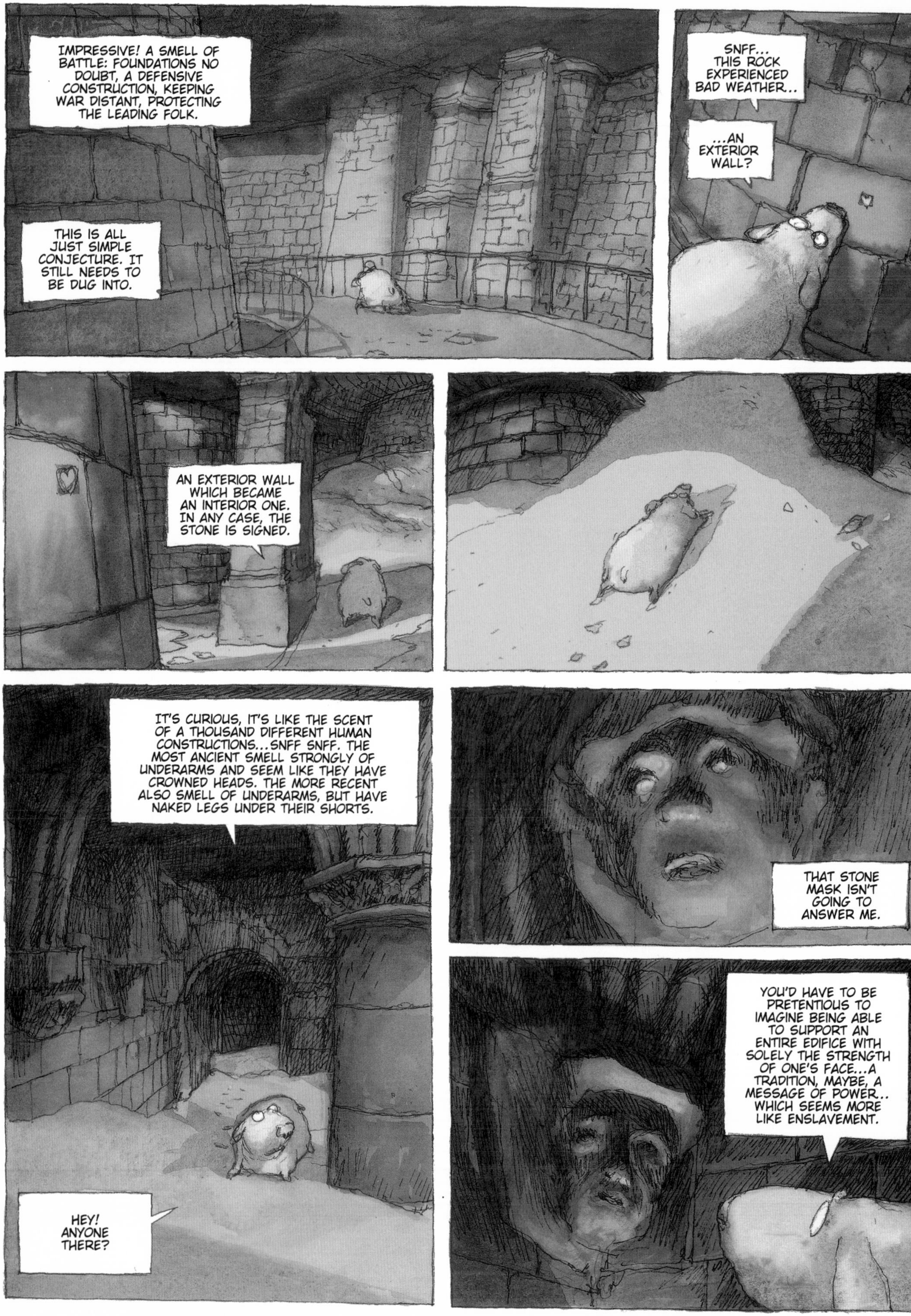
IMPRESSIVE! A SMELL OF BATTLE: FOUNDATIONS NO DOUBT, A DEFENSIVE CONSTRUCTION, KEEPING WAR DISTANT, PROTECTING THE LEADING FOLK.
THIS IS ALL JUST SIMPLE CONJECTURE. IT STILL NEEDS TO BE DUG INTO.
SNFF... THIS ROCK EXPERIENCED BAD WEATHER...
...AN EXTERIOR WALL?
AN EXTERIOR WALL WHICH BECAME AN INTERIOR ONE. IN ANY CASE, THE STONE IS SIGNED.
IT'S CURIOUS, IT'S LIKE THE SCENT OF A THOUSAND DIFFERENT HUMAN CONSTRUCTIONS...SNFF SNFF. THE MOST ANCIENT SMELL STRONGLY OF UNDERARMS AND SEEM LIKE THEY HAVE CROWNED HEADS. THE MORE RECENT ALSO SMELL OF UNDERARMS, BUT HAVE NAKED LEGS UNDER THEIR SHORTS.
HEY! ANYONE THERE?
THAT STONE MASK ISN'T GOING TO ANSWER ME.
YOU'D HAVE TO BE PRETENTIOUS TO IMAGINE BEING ABLE TO SUPPORT AN ENTIRE EDIFICE WITH SOLELY THE STRENGTH OF ONE'S FACE...A TRADITION, MAYBE, A MESSAGE OF POWER... WHICH SEEMS MORE LIKE ENSLAVEMENT.

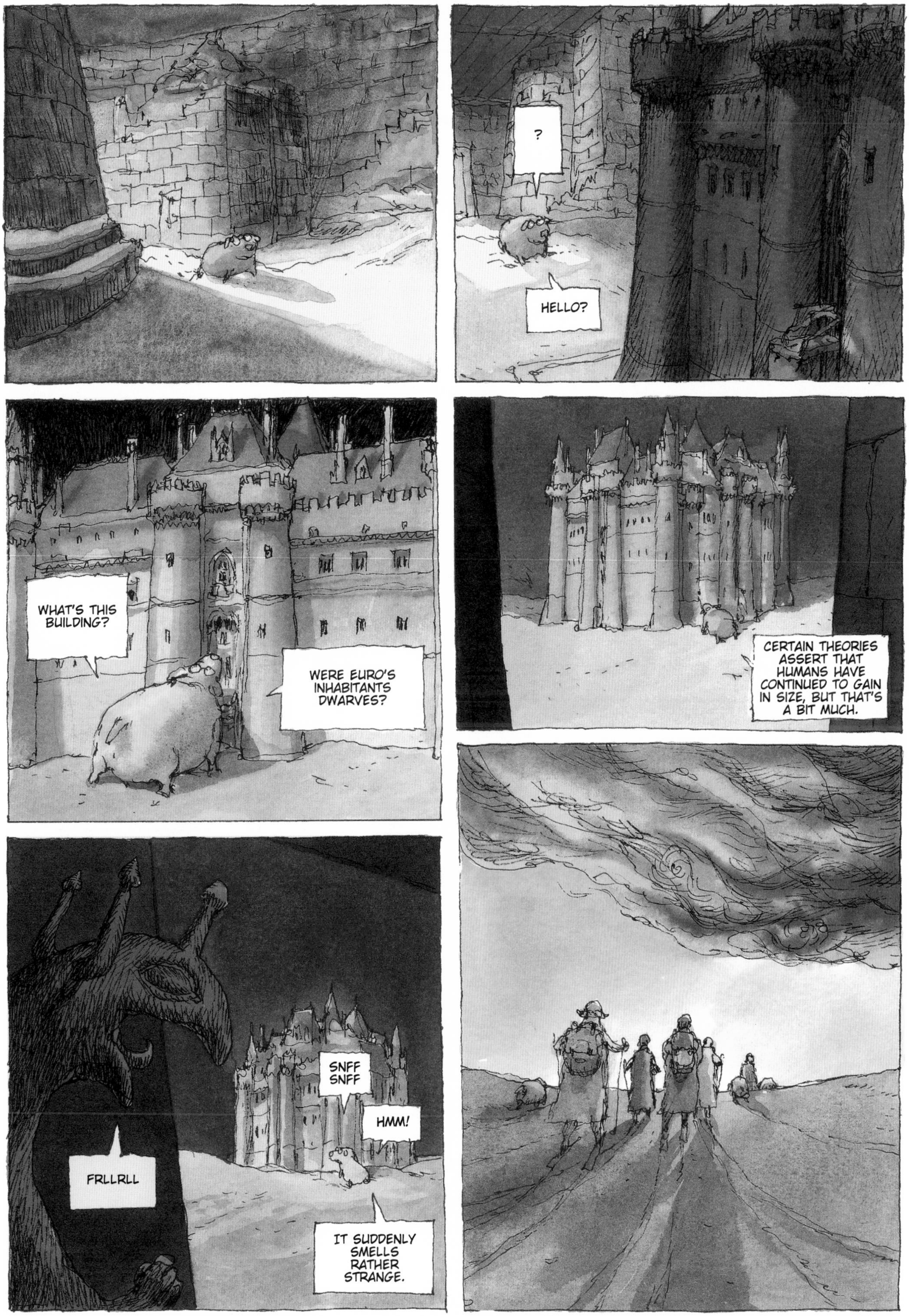
?
HELLO?
WHAT'S THIS BUILDING?
WERE EURO'S INHABITANTS DWARVES?
CERTAIN THEORIES ASSERT THAT HUMANS HAVE CONTINUED TO GAIN IN SIZE, BUT THAT'S A BIT MUCH.
SNFF SNFF
HMM!
FRLLRLL
IT SUDDENLY SMELLS RATHER STRANGE.

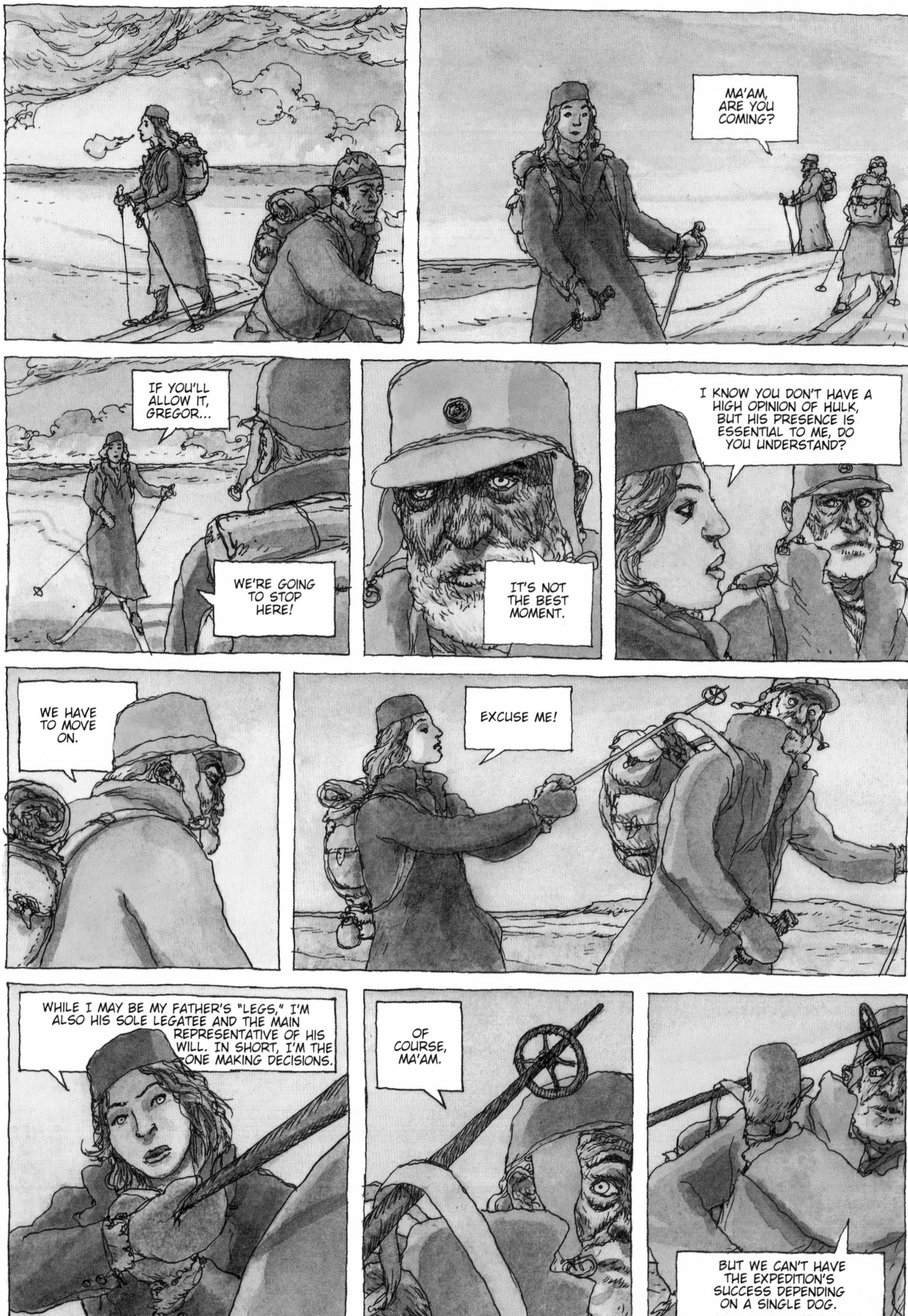
MA'AM, ARE YOU COMING?
IF YOU'LL ALLOW IT, GREGOR...
WE'RE GOING TO STOP HERE!
IT'S NOT THE BEST MOMENT.
I KNOW YOU DON'T HAVE A HIGH OPINION OF HULK, BUT HIS PRESENCE IS ESSENTIAL TO ME, DO YOU UNDERSTAND?
WE HAVE TO MOVE ON.
EXCUSE ME!
WHILE I MAY BE MY FATHER'S "LEGS," I'M ALSO HIS SOLE LEGATEE AND THE MAIN REPRESENTATIVE OF HIS WILL. IN SHORT, I'M THE ONE MAKING DECISIONS.
OF COURSE, MA'AM.
BUT WE CAN'T HAVE THE EXPEDITION'S SUCCESS DEPENDING ON A SINGLE DOG.

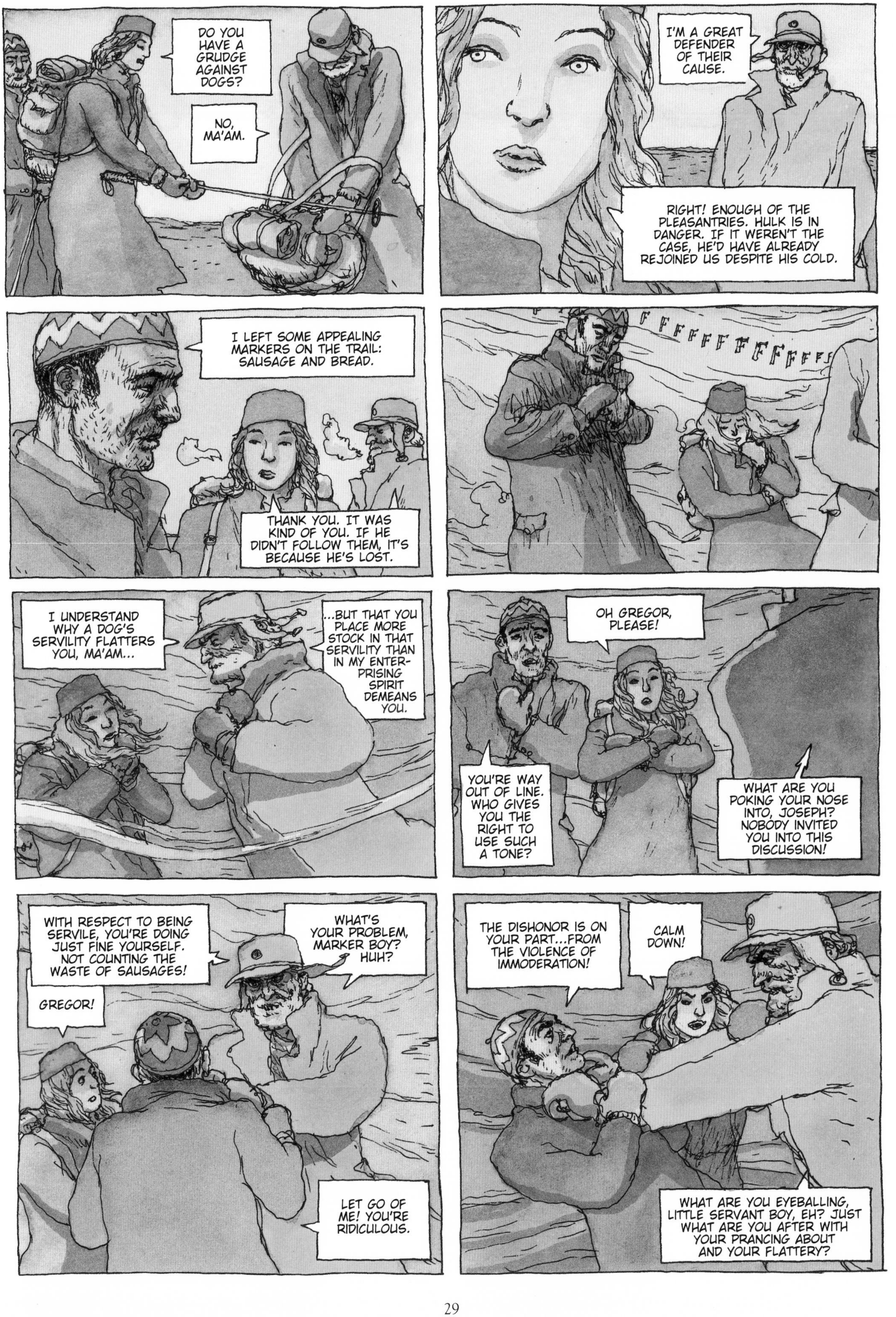
DO YOU HAVE A GRUDGE AGAINST DOGS?
NO, MA'AM.
I'M A GREAT DEFENDER OF THEIR CAUSE.
RIGHT! ENOUGH OF THE PLEASANTRIES. HULK IS IN DANGER. IF IT WEREN'T THE CASE, HE'D HAVE ALREADY REJOINED US DESPITE HIS COLD.
I LEFT SOME APPEALING MARKERS ON THE TRAIL: SAUSAGE AND BREAD.
THANK YOU. IT WAS KIND OF YOU. IF HE DIDN'T FOLLOW THEM, IT'S BECAUSE HE'S LOST.
FFFFFFFFFFFFFF
I UNDERSTAND WHY A DOG'S SERVILITY FLATTERS YOU, MA'AM...
...BUT THAT YOU PLACE MORE STOCK IN THAT SERVILITY THAN IN MY ENTER-PRISING SPIRIT DEMEANS YOU.
OH GREGOR, PLEASE!
YOU'RE WAY OUT OF LINE. WHO GIVES YOU THE RIGHT TO USE SUCH A TONE?
WHAT ARE YOU POKING YOUR NOSE INTO, JOSEPH? NOBODY INVITED YOU INTO THIS DISCUSSION!
WITH RESPECT TO BEING SERVILE, YOU'RE DOING JUST FINE YOURSELF. NOT COUNTING THE WASTE OF SAUSAGES!
WHAT'S YOUR PROBLEM, MARKER BOY? HUH?
GREGOR!
LET GO OF ME! YOU'RE RIDICULOUS.
THE DISHONOR IS ON YOUR PART...FROM THE VIOLENCE OF IMMODERATION!
CALM DOWN!
WHAT ARE YOU EYEBALLING, LITTLE SERVANT BOY, EH? JUST WHAT ARE YOU AFTER WITH YOUR PRANCING ABOUT AND YOUR FLATTERY?

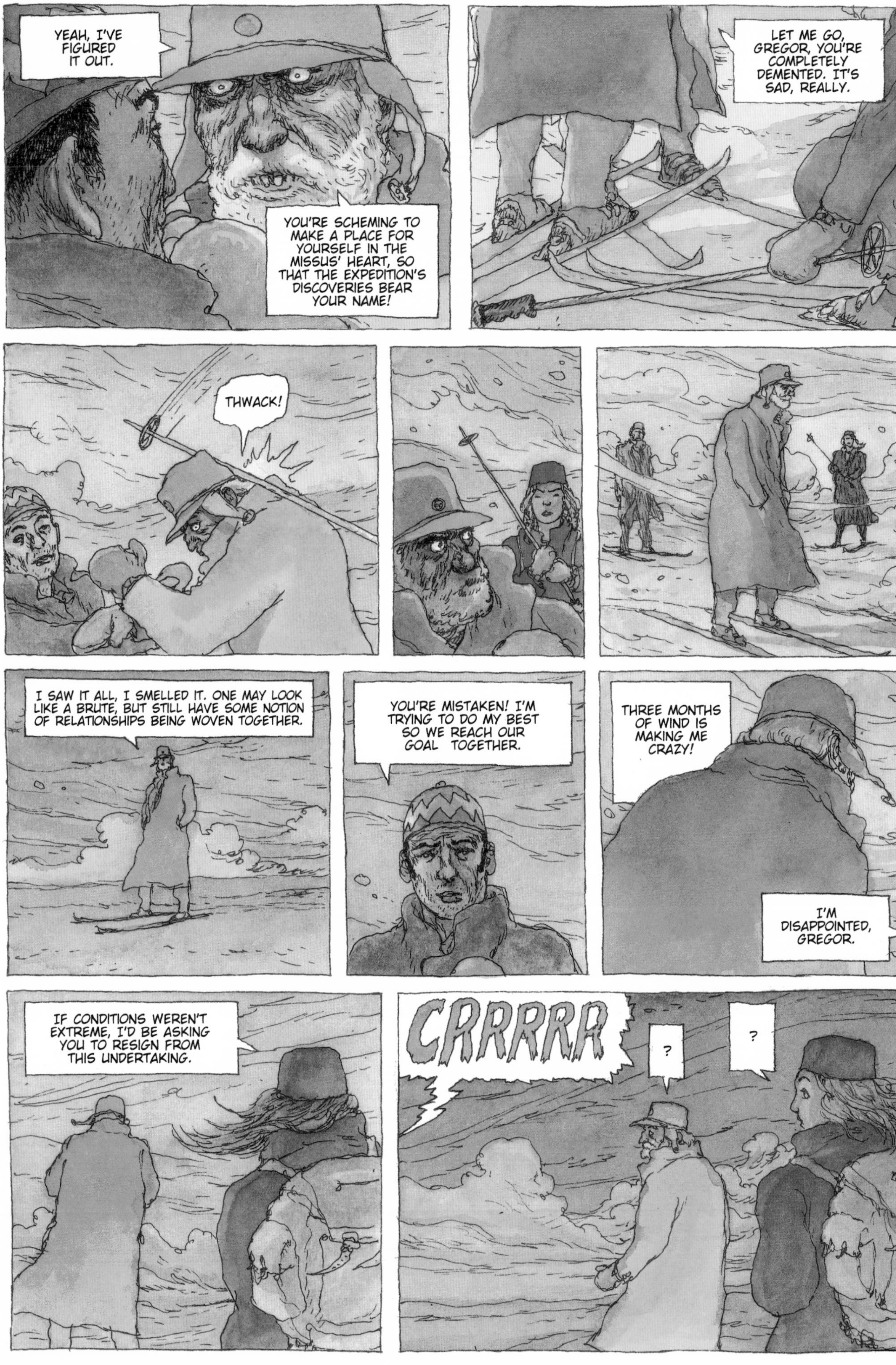

YEAH, I'VE FIGURED IT OUT.
YOU'RE SCHEMING TO MAKE A PLACE FOR YOURSELF IN THE MISSUS' HEART, SO THAT THE EXPEDITION'S DISCOVERIES BEAR YOUR NAME!
LET ME GO, GREGOR, YOU'RE COMPLETELY DEMENTED. IT'S SAD, REALLY.
THWACK!
I SAW IT ALL, I SMELLED IT. ONE MAY LOOK LIKE A BRUTE, BUT STILL HAVE SOME NOTION OF RELATIONSHIPS BEING WOVEN TOGETHER.
YOU'RE MISTAKEN! I'M TRYING TO DO MY BEST SO WE REACH OUR GOAL TOGETHER.
THREE MONTHS OF WIND IS MAKING ME CRAZY!
I'M DISAPPOINTED, GREGOR.
IF CONDITIONS WEREN'T EXTREME, I'D BE ASKING YOU TO RESIGN FROM THIS UNDERTAKING.
CRRRRR
?
?

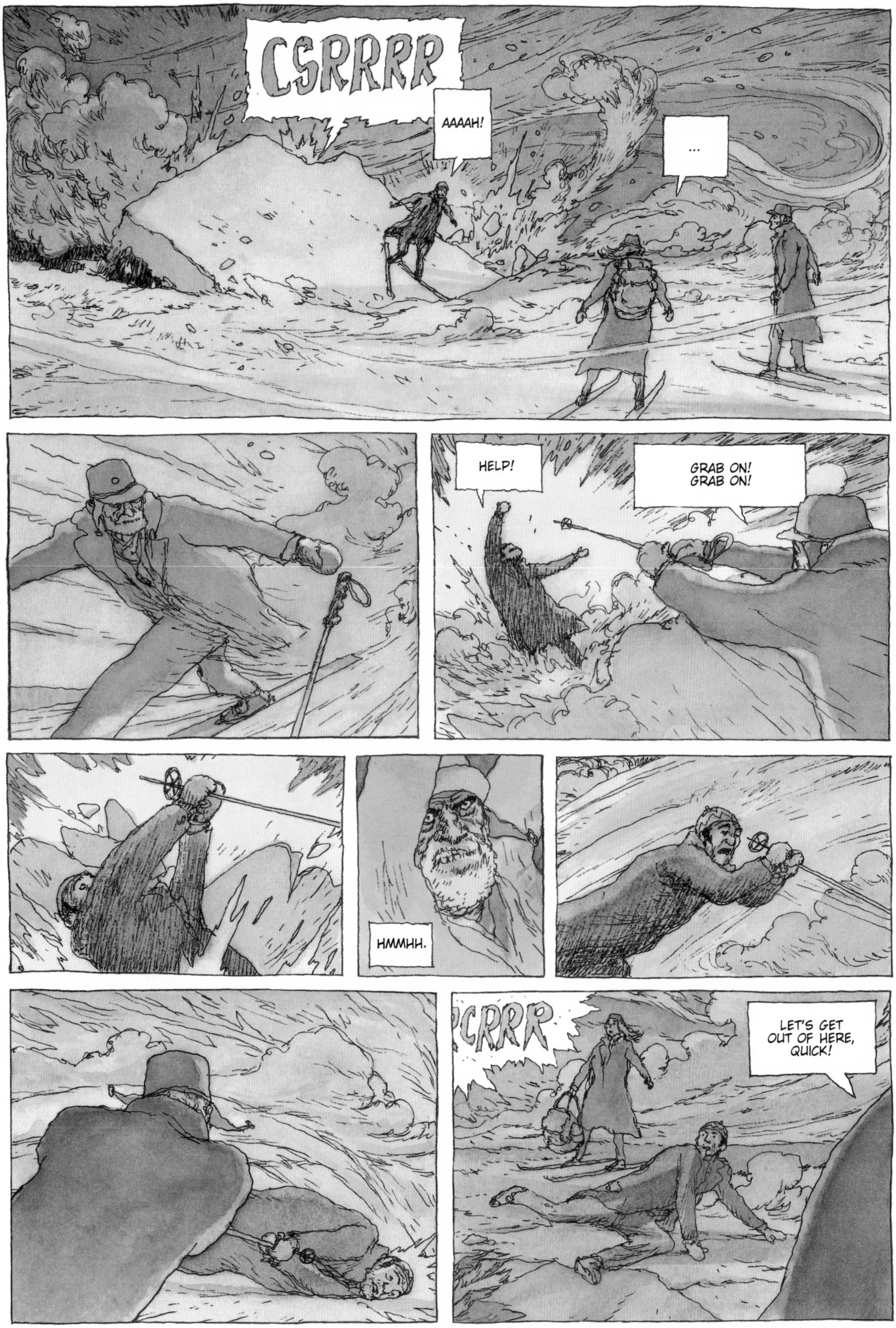
CSRRRR
AAAAH!
...
HELP!
GRAB ON! GRAB ON!
HMMHH.
CRRR
LET'S GET OUT OF HERE, QUICK!

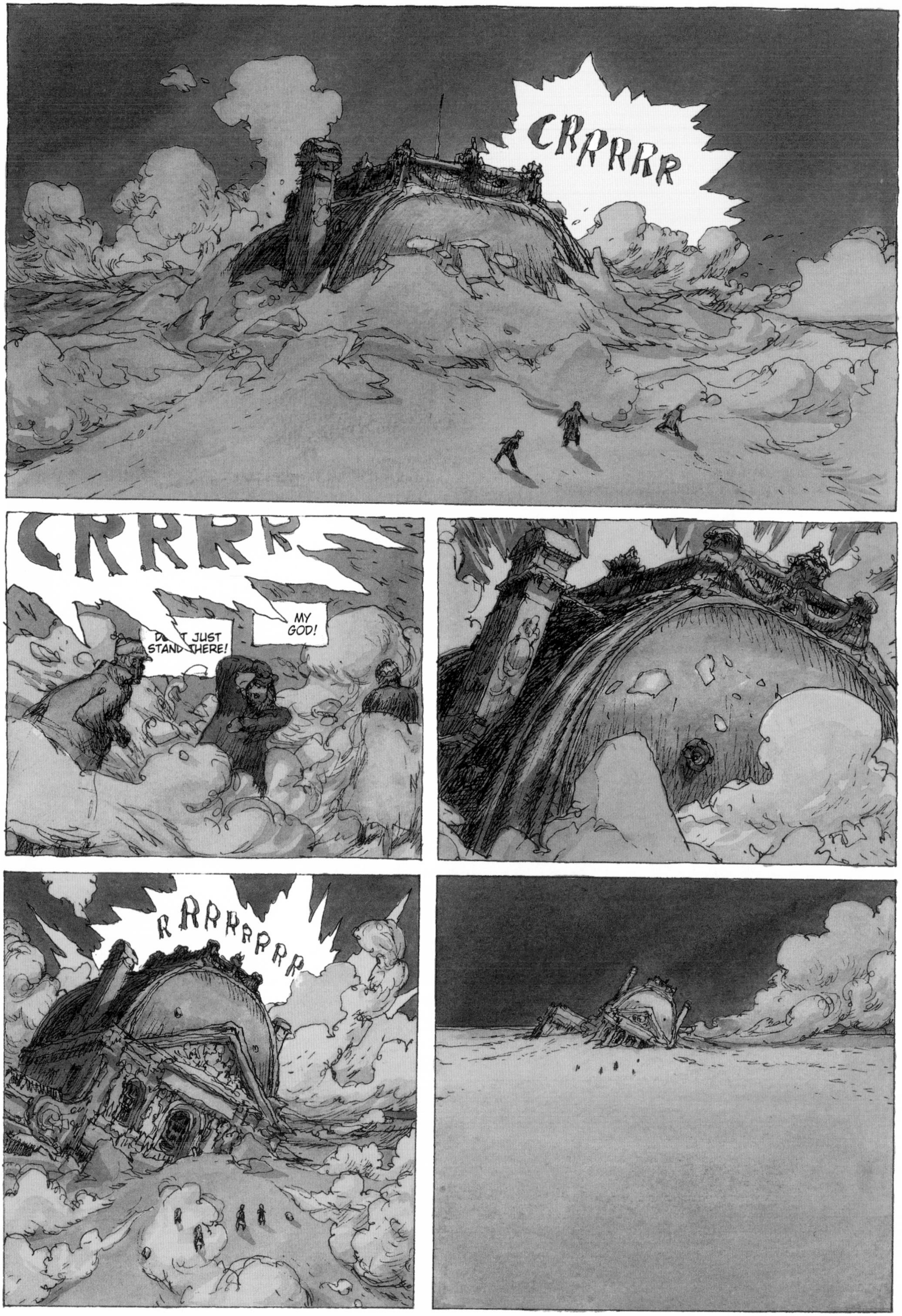
CRRRRRR
CRRRR
DON'T JUST STAND THERE!
MY GOD!
R RRRRRRRRR

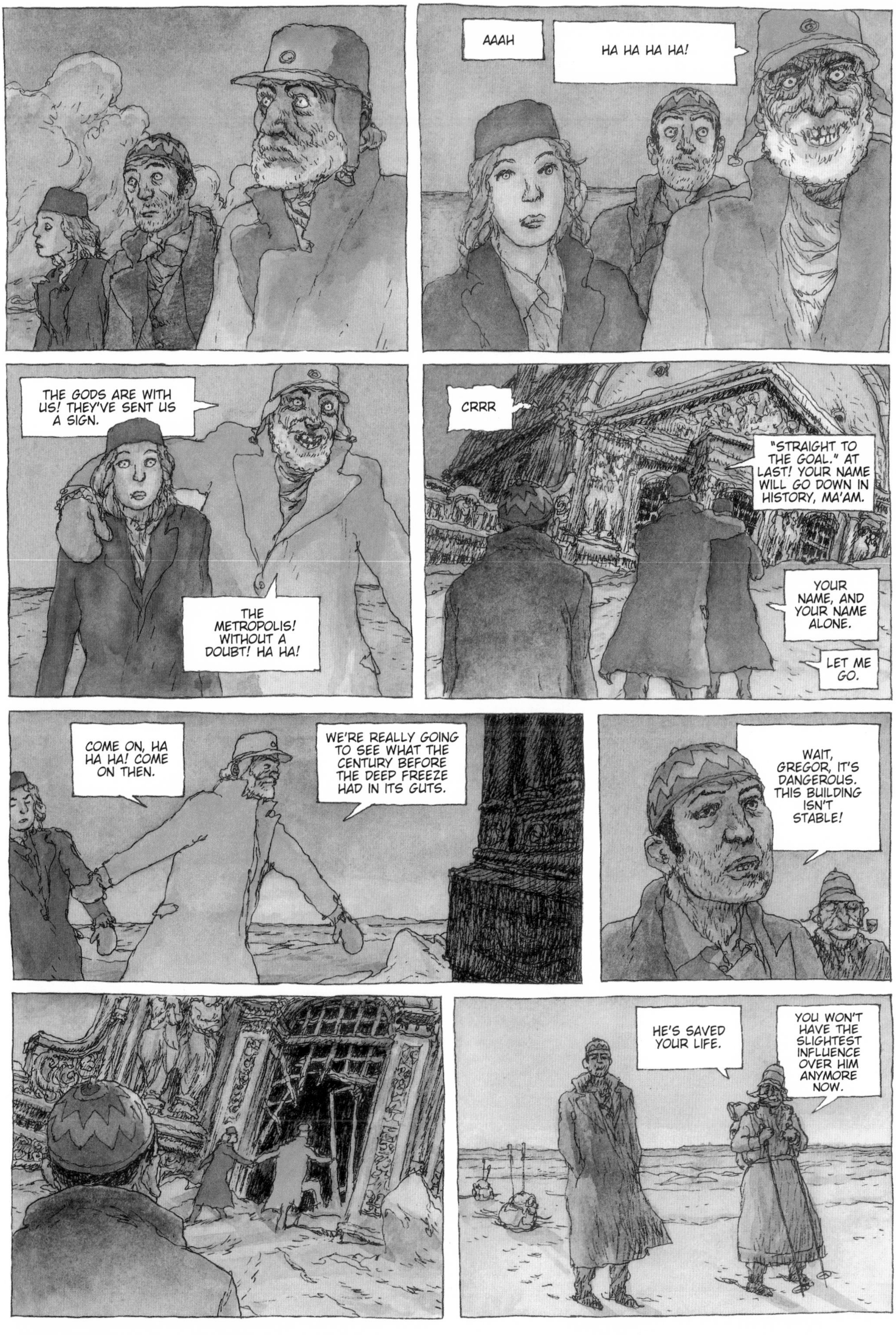
AAAH
HA HA HA HA!
THE GODS ARE WITH US! THEY'VE SENT US A SIGN.
THE METROPOLIS! WITHOUT A DOUBT! HA HA!
CRRR
"STRAIGHT TO THE GOAL." AT LAST! YOUR NAME WILL GO DOWN IN HISTORY, MA'AM.
YOUR NAME, AND YOUR NAME ALONE.
LET ME GO.
COME ON, HA HA HA! COME ON THEN.
WE'RE REALLY GOING TO SEE WHAT THE CENTURY BEFORE THE DEEP FREEZE HAD IN ITS GUTS.
WAIT, GREGOR, IT'S DANGEROUS. THIS BUILDING ISN'T STABLE!
HE'S SAVED YOUR LIFE.
YOU WON'T HAVE THE SLIGHTEST INFLUENCE OVER HIM ANYMORE NOW.

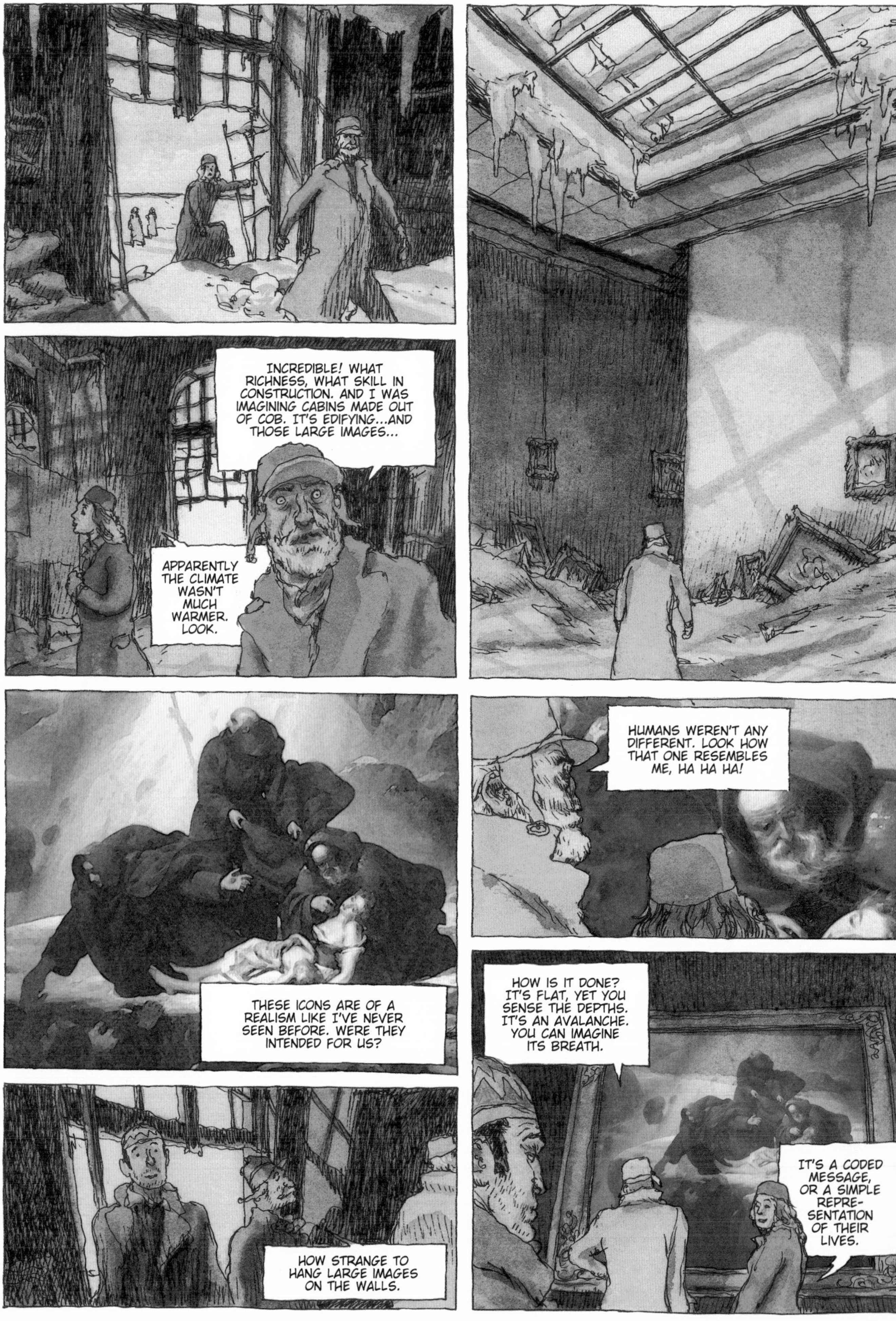
INCREDIBLE! WHAT RICHNESS, WHAT SKILL IN CONSTRUCTION. AND I WAS IMAGINING CABINS MADE OUT OF COB. IT'S EDIFYING...AND THOSE LARGE IMAGES...
APPARENTLY THE CLIMATE WASN'T MUCH WARMER. LOOK.
THESE ICONS ARE OF A REALISM LIKE I'VE NEVER SEEN BEFORE. WERE THEY INTENDED FOR US?
HOW STRANGE TO HANG LARGE IMAGES ON THE WALLS.
HUMANS WEREN'T ANY DIFFERENT. LOOK HOW THAT ONE RESEMBLES ME, HA HA HA!
HOW IS IT DONE? IT'S FLAT, YET YOU SENSE THE DEPTHS. IT'S AN AVALANCHE. YOU CAN IMAGINE ITS BREATH.
IT'S A CODED MESSAGE, OR A SIMPLE REPRE-SENTATION OF THEIR LIVES.

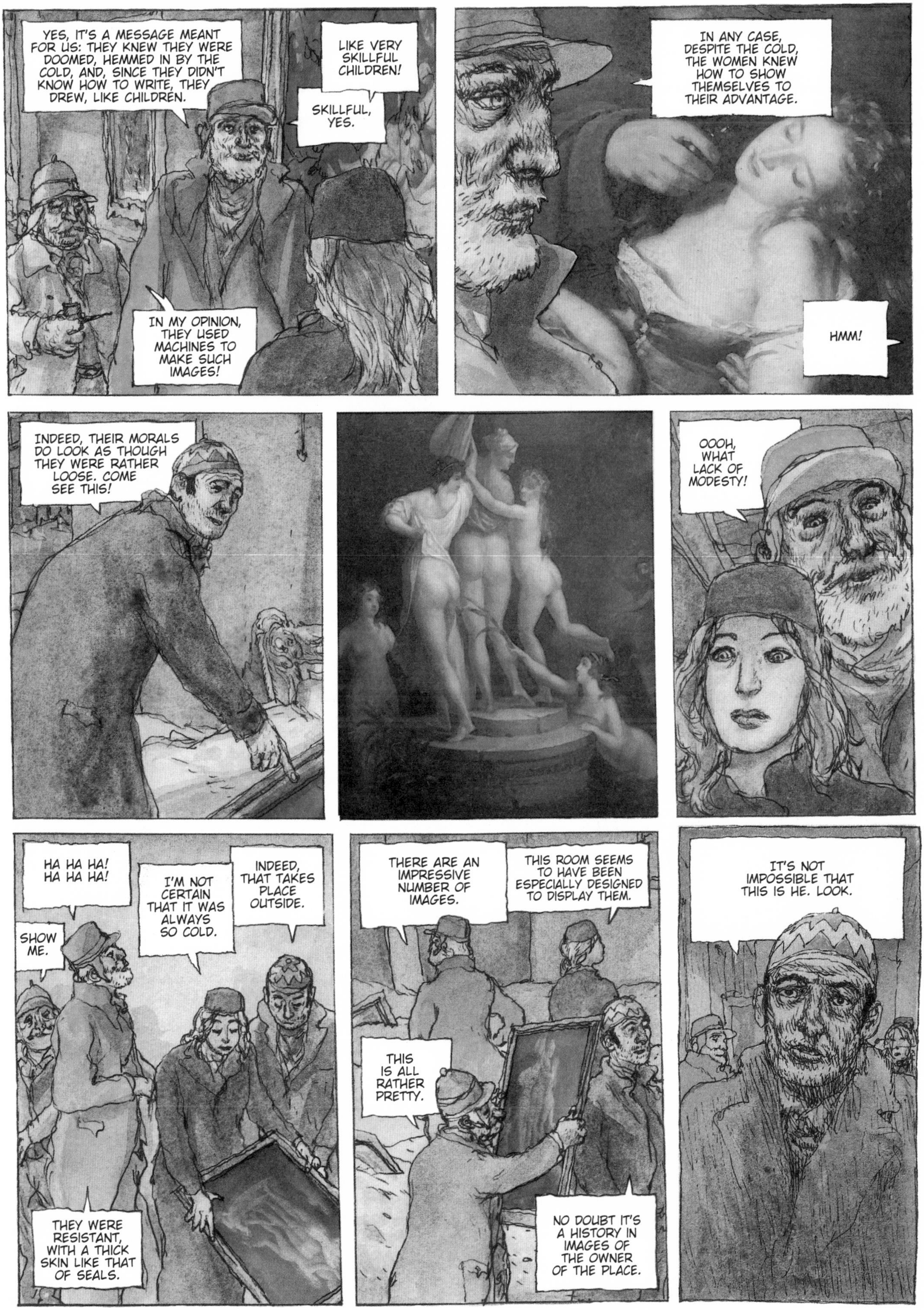
YES, IT'S A MESSAGE MEANT FOR US: THEY KNEW THEY WERE DOOMED, HEMMED IN BY THE COLD, AND, SINCE THEY DIDN'T KNOW HOW TO WRITE, THEY DREW, LIKE CHILDREN.
LIKE VERY SKILLFUL CHILDREN!
SKILLFUL, YES.
IN MY OPINION, THEY USED MACHINES TO MAKE SUCH IMAGES!
IN ANY CASE, DESPITE THE COLD, THE WOMEN KNEW HOW TO SHOW THEMSELVES TO THEIR ADVANTAGE.
HMM!
INDEED, THEIR MORALS DO LOOK AS THOUGH THEY WERE RATHER LOOSE. COME SEE THIS!
OOOH, WHAT LACK OF MODESTY!
HA HA HA! HA HA HA!
SHOW ME.
I'M NOT CERTAIN THAT IT WAS ALWAYS SO COLD.
INDEED, THAT TAKES PLACE OUTSIDE.
THEY WERE RESISTANT, WITH A THICK SKIN LIKE THAT OF SEALS.
THERE ARE AN IMPRESSIVE NUMBER OF IMAGES.
THIS ROOM SEEMS TO HAVE BEEN ESPECIALLY DESIGNED TO DISPLAY THEM.
THIS IS ALL RATHER PRETTY.
NO DOUBT IT'S A HISTORY IN IMAGES OF THE OWNER OF THE PLACE.
IT'S NOT IMPOSSIBLE THAT THIS IS HE. LOOK.

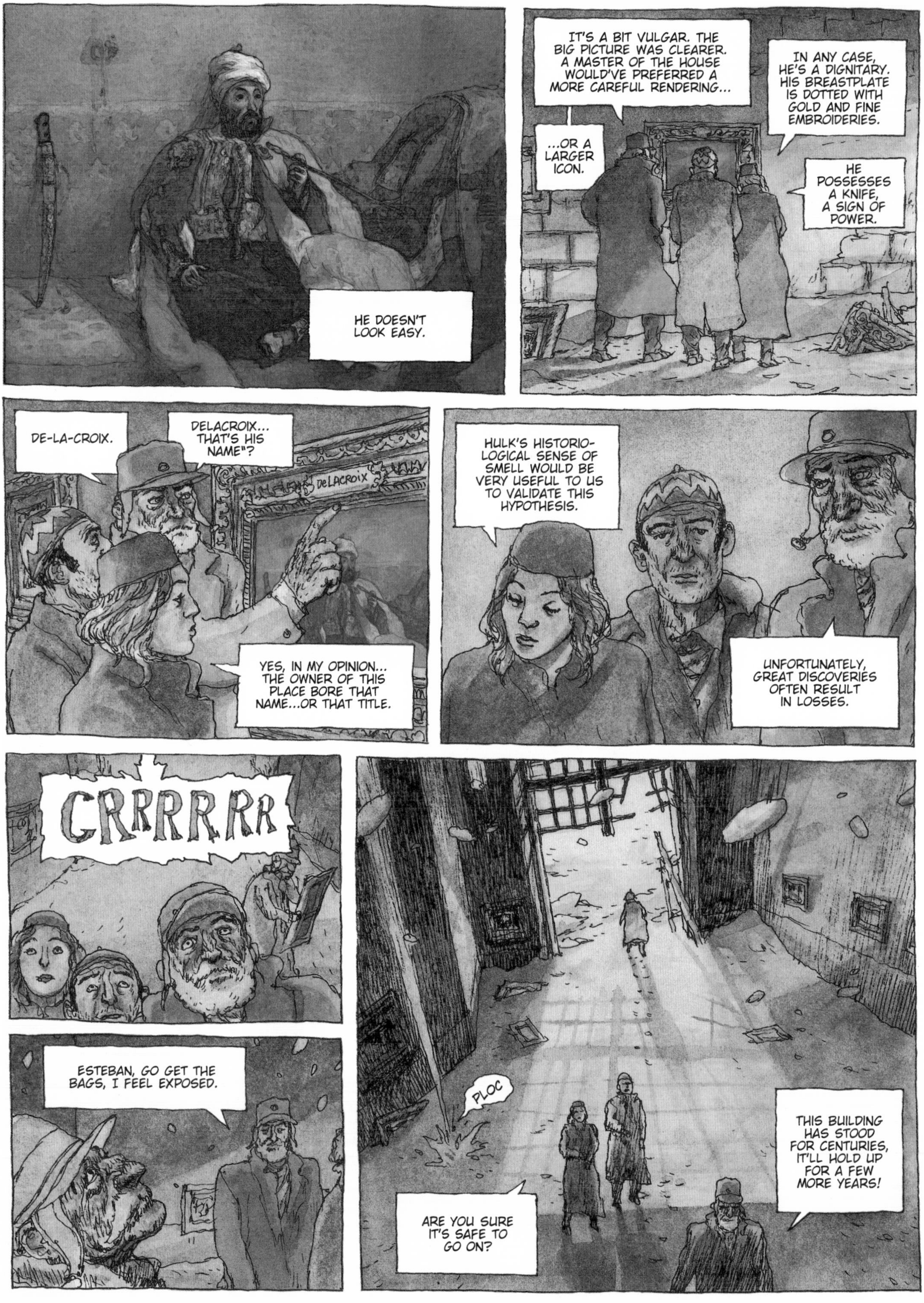
HE DOESN'T LOOK EASY.
IT'S A BIT VULGAR. THE BIG PICTURE WAS CLEARER. A MASTER OF THE HOUSE WOULD'VE PREFERRED A MORE CAREFUL RENDERING...
...OR A LARGER ICON.
IN ANY CASE, HE'S A DIGNITARY. HIS BREASTPLATE IS DOTTED WITH GOLD AND FINE EMBROIDERIES.
HE POSSESSES A KNIFE, A SIGN OF POWER.
DE-LA-CROIX.
DELACROIX... THAT'S HIS NAME"?
DeLACROIX
YES, IN MY OPINION... THE OWNER OF THIS PLACE BORE THAT NAME...OR THAT TITLE.
HULK'S HISTORIO-LOGICAL SENSE OF SMELL WOULD BE VERY USEFUL TO US TO VALIDATE THIS HYPOTHESIS.
UNFORTUNATELY, GREAT DISCOVERIES OFTEN RESULT IN LOSSES.
CRRRRRR
ESTEBAN, GO GET THE BAGS, I FEEL EXPOSED.
PLOC
ARE YOU SURE IT'S SAFE TO GO ON?
THIS BUILDING HAS STOOD FOR CENTURIES, IT'LL HOLD UP FOR A FEW MORE YEARS!

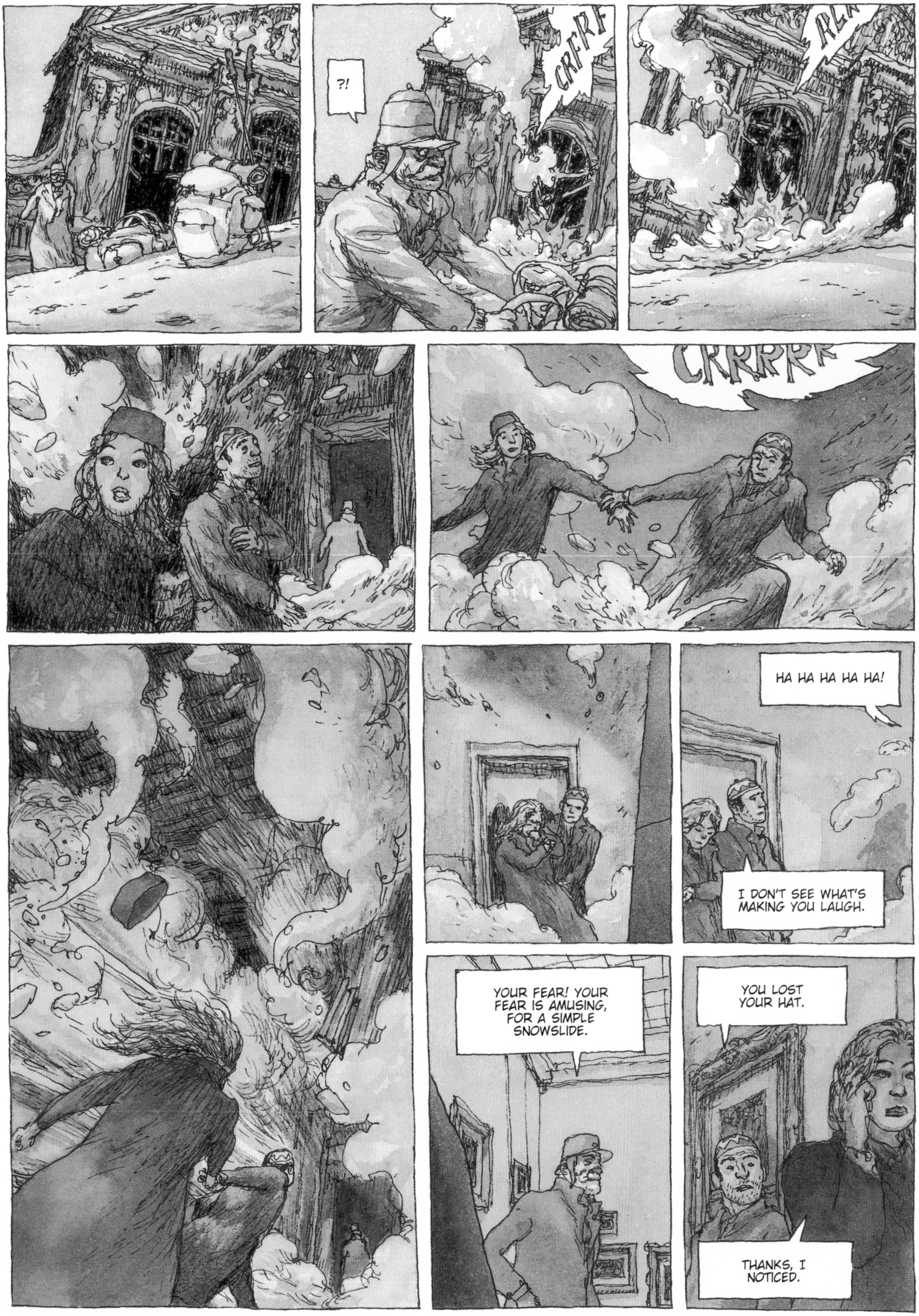
?!
CRFRF
CRRRRF
HA HA HA HA HA!
I DON'T SEE WHAT'S MAKING YOU LAUGH.
YOUR FEAR! YOUR FEAR IS AMUSING, FOR A SIMPLE SNOWSLIDE.
YOU LOST YOUR HAT.
THANKS, I NOTICED.

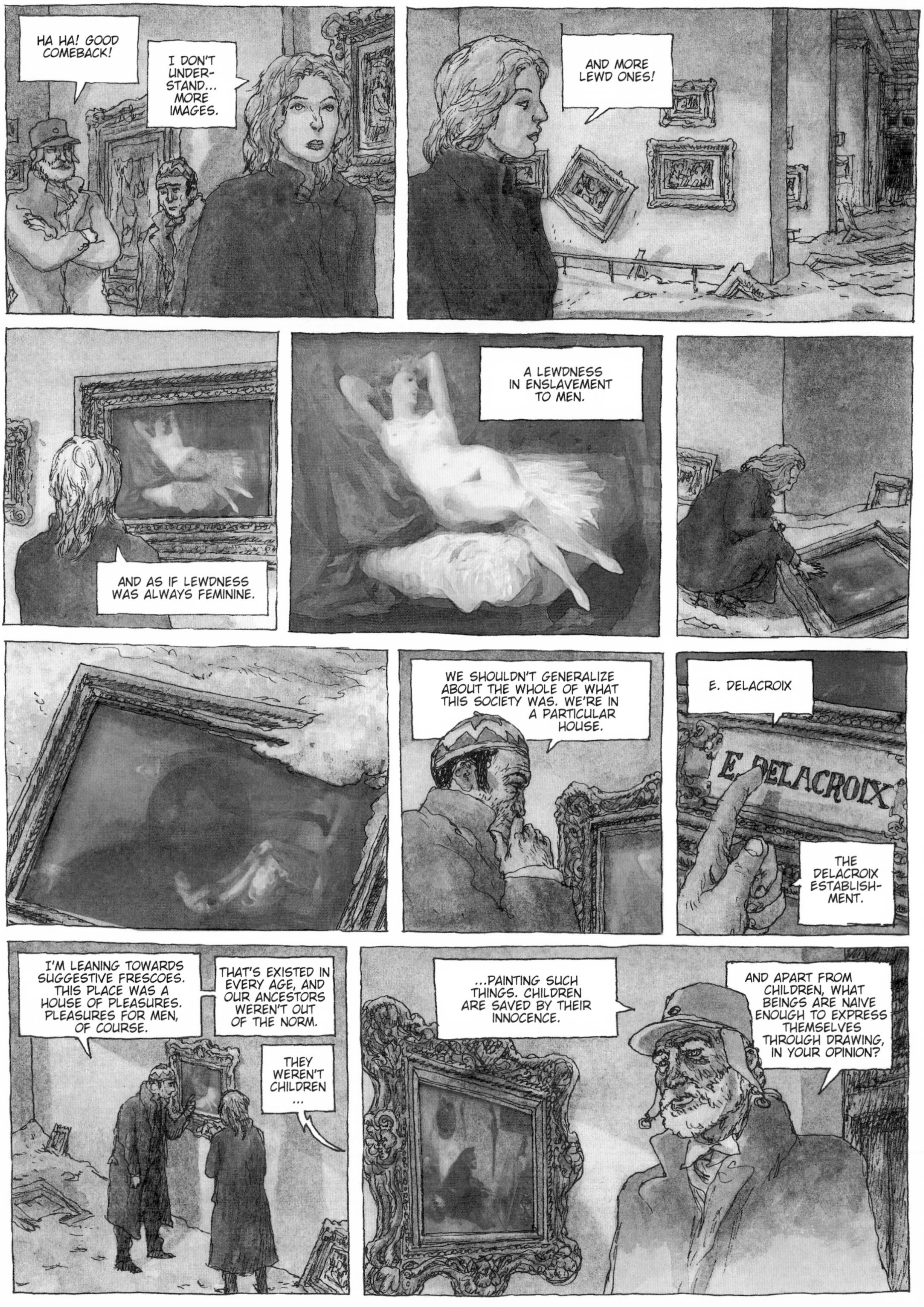
HA HA! GOOD COMEBACK!
I DON'T UNDER-STAND... MORE IMAGES.
AND MORE LEWD ONES!
AND AS IF LEWDNESS WAS ALWAYS FEMININE.
A LEWDNESS IN ENSLAVEMENT TO MEN.
WE SHOULDN'T GENERALIZE ABOUT THE WHOLE OF WHAT THIS SOCIETY WAS. WE'RE IN A PARTICULAR HOUSE.
E. DELACROIX
E. DELACROIX
THE DELACROIX ESTABLISH-MENT.
I'M LEANING TOWARDS SUGGESTIVE FRESCOES. THIS PLACE WAS A HOUSE OF PLEASURES. PLEASURES FOR MEN, OF COURSE.
THAT'S EXISTED IN EVERY AGE, AND OUR ANCESTORS WEREN'T OUT OF THE NORM.
THEY WEREN'T CHILDREN ...
...PAINTING SUCH THINGS. CHILDREN ARE SAVED BY THEIR INNOCENCE.
AND APART FROM CHILDREN, WHAT BEINGS ARE NAIVE ENOUGH TO EXPRESS THEMSELVES THROUGH DRAWING, IN YOUR OPINION?

IT'S FOR ANIMALS, NO DOUBT, TO TRANSLATE ALL THE BESTIALITY OF CARNAL ATTRACTION.

WHO BETTER THAN A MONKEY CAN EXALT THE CRUDE? WITH FRONTAL IMAGES WITH NO THOUGHT OR METAPHOR.

I'M NOT CERTAIN AN ANIMAL WOULD BE CAPABLE OF DRAWING, EVEN IF IT WANTED TO EXPRESS ITSELF AND DIDN'T KNOW HOW TO WRITE.

HULK'S AN ANIMAL AS FAR AS I CAN TELL!

HIS SENSE OF SMELL DECRYPTS HISTORICAL CONTINUITY! HE'D BE ABLE TO DRAW!

YOU KNOW FULL WELL HULK AND HIS KIND ARE GENETICALLY MODIFIED, AND THAT SUCH MODIFICATIONS DIDN'T EXIST IN THAT ERA.

WHO KNOWS?

IN ANY CASE, ONE THING IS OBVIOUS: THIS CIVILIZATION WASN'T LITERARY. HAVE YOU SEEN ANYTHING THAT DEMONSTRATES THAT?

WE'VE NOT SEEN EVERYTHING.

IT WASN'T LITERARY, BUT ORAL AND ICONOGRAPHIC. IMAGERY IS PREHISTORIC.

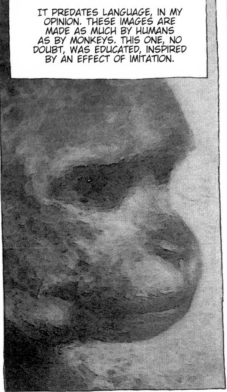

IT PREDATES LANGUAGE, IN MY OPINION. THESE IMAGES ARE MADE AS MUCH BY HUMANS AS BY MONKEYS. THIS ONE, NO DOUBT, WAS EDUCATED, INSPIRED BY AN EFFECT OF IMITATION.

HOW CAN ONE LIVE WITH IMAGES AS THE SOLE SOURCE OF OUTLOOK? OUR ANCESTORS WERE FRUSTRATED!

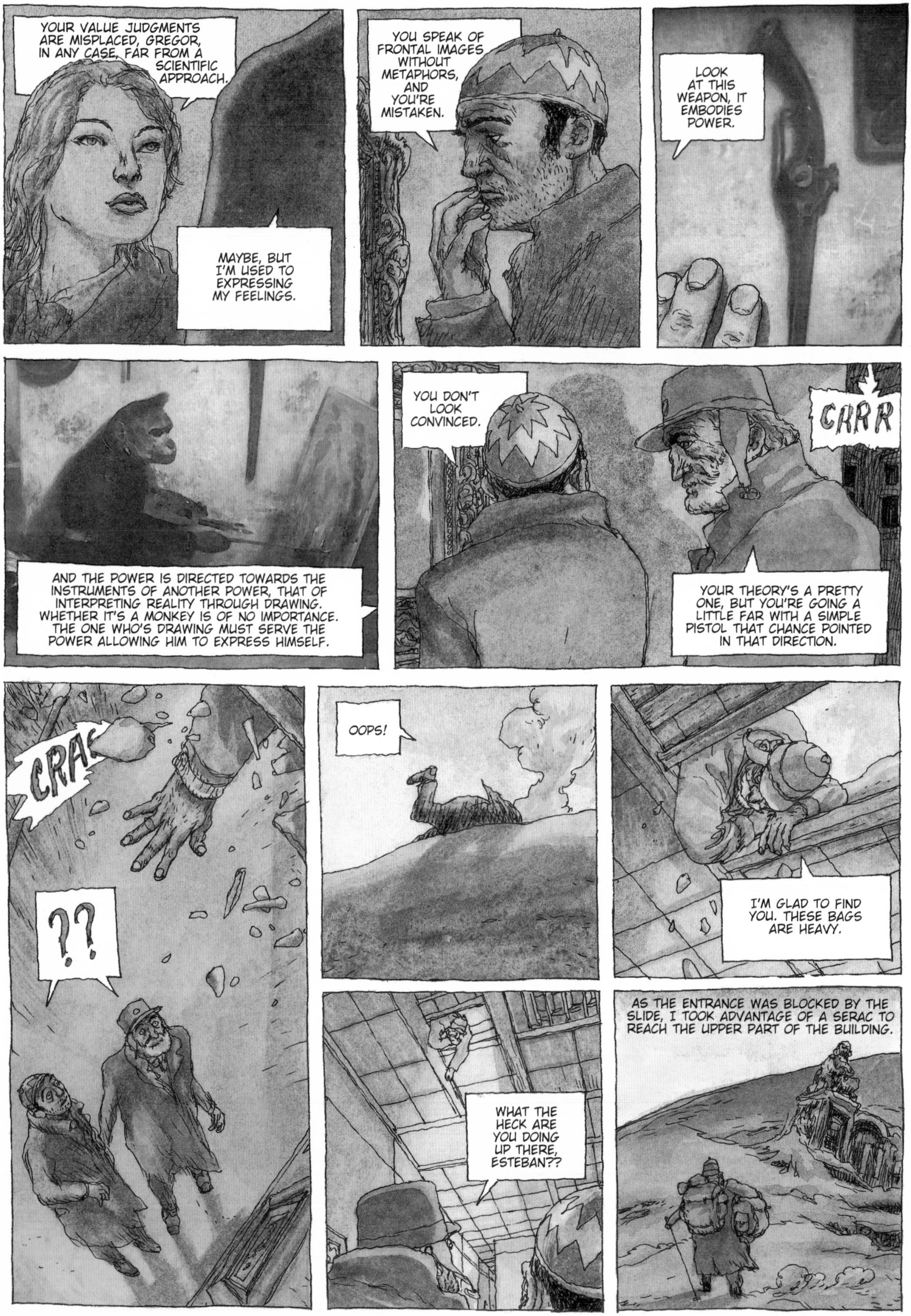
YOUR VALUE JUDGMENTS ARE MISPLACED, GREGOR, IN ANY CASE, FAR FROM A SCIENTIFIC APPROACH.
MAYBE, BUT I'M USED TO EXPRESSING MY FEELINGS.
YOU SPEAK OF FRONTAL IMAGES WITHOUT METAPHORS, AND YOU'RE MISTAKEN.
LOOK AT THIS WEAPON, IT EMBODIES POWER.
AND THE POWER IS DIRECTED TOWARDS THE INSTRUMENTS OF ANOTHER POWER, THAT OF INTERPRETING REALITY THROUGH DRAWING. WHETHER IT'S A MONKEY IS OF NO IMPORTANCE. THE ONE WHO'S DRAWING MUST SERVE THE POWER ALLOWING HIM TO EXPRESS HIMSELF.
YOU DON'T LOOK CONVINCED.
CRRR
YOUR THEORY'S A PRETTY ONE, BUT YOU'RE GOING A LITTLE FAR WITH A SIMPLE PISTOL THAT CHANCE POINTED IN THAT DIRECTION.
CRA
??
OOPS!
I'M GLAD TO FIND YOU. THESE BAGS ARE HEAVY.
WHAT THE HECK ARE YOU DOING UP THERE, ESTEBAN??
AS THE ENTRANCE WAS BLOCKED BY THE SLIDE, I TOOK ADVANTAGE OF A SERAC TO REACH THE UPPER PART OF THE BUILDING.

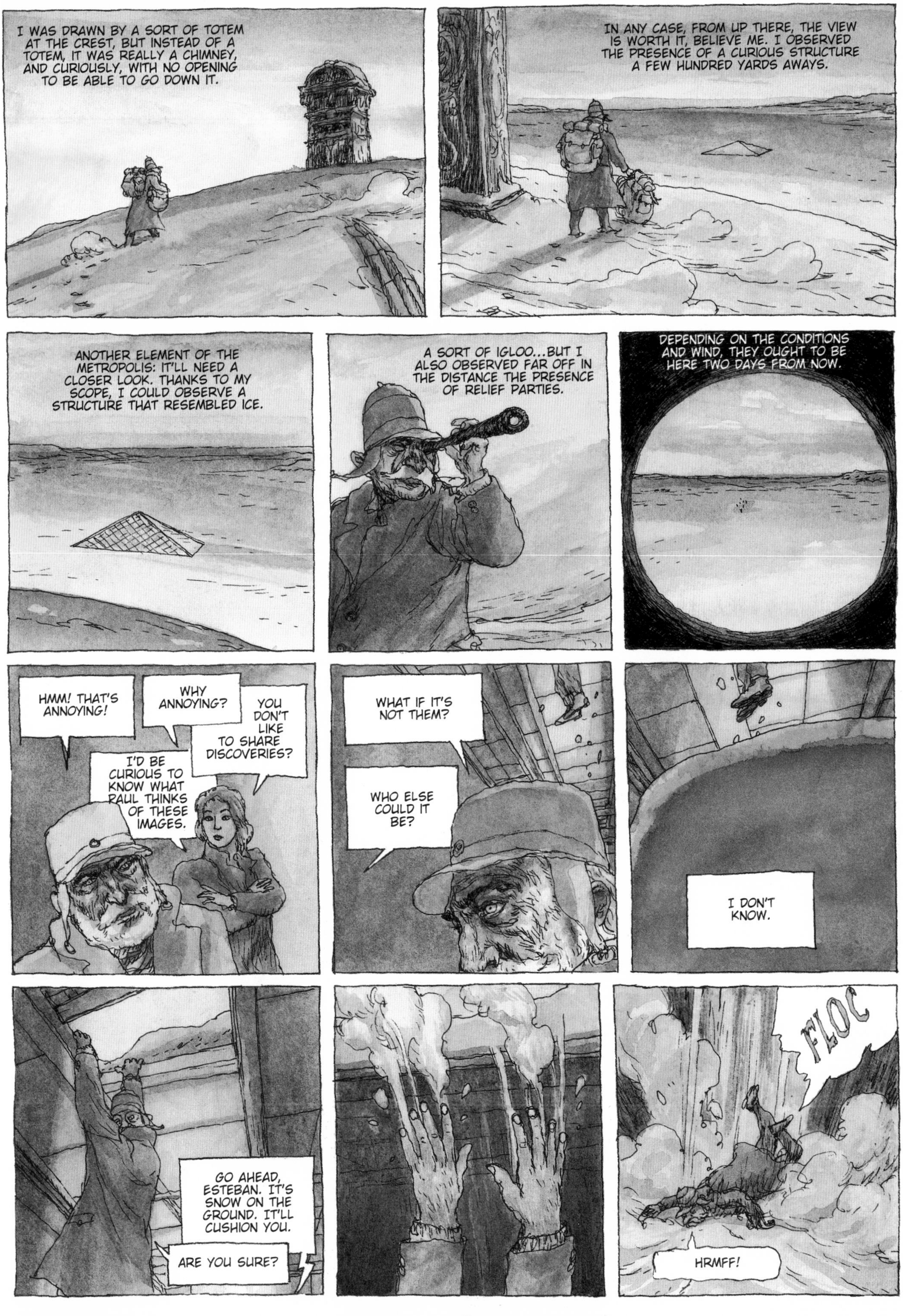
I WAS DRAWN BY A SORT OF TOTEM AT THE CREST, BUT INSTEAD OF A TOTEM, IT WAS REALLY A CHIMNEY, AND CURIOUSLY, WITH NO OPENING TO BE ABLE TO GO DOWN IT.
IN ANY CASE, FROM UP THERE, THE VIEW IS WORTH IT, BELIEVE ME. I OBSERVED THE PRESENCE OF A CURIOUS STRUCTURE A FEW HUNDRED YARDS AWAYS.
ANOTHER ELEMENT OF THE METROPOLIS: IT'LL NEED A CLOSER LOOK. THANKS TO MY SCOPE, I COULD OBSERVE A STRUCTURE THAT RESEMBLED ICE.
A SORT OF IGLOO...BUT I ALSO OBSERVED FAR OFF IN THE DISTANCE THE PRESENCE OF RELIEF PARTIES.
DEPENDING ON THE CONDITIONS AND WIND, THEY OUGHT TO BE HERE TWO DAYS FROM NOW.
HMM! THAT'S ANNOYING!
WHY ANNOYING?
YOU DON'T LIKE TO SHARE DISCOVERIES?
I'D BE CURIOUS TO KNOW WHAT PAUL THINKS OF THESE IMAGES.
WHAT IF IT'S NOT THEM?
WHO ELSE COULD IT BE?
I DON'T KNOW.
GO AHEAD, ESTEBAN. IT'S SNOW ON THE GROUND. IT'LL CUSHION YOU.
ARE YOU SURE?
FLOC
HRMFF!

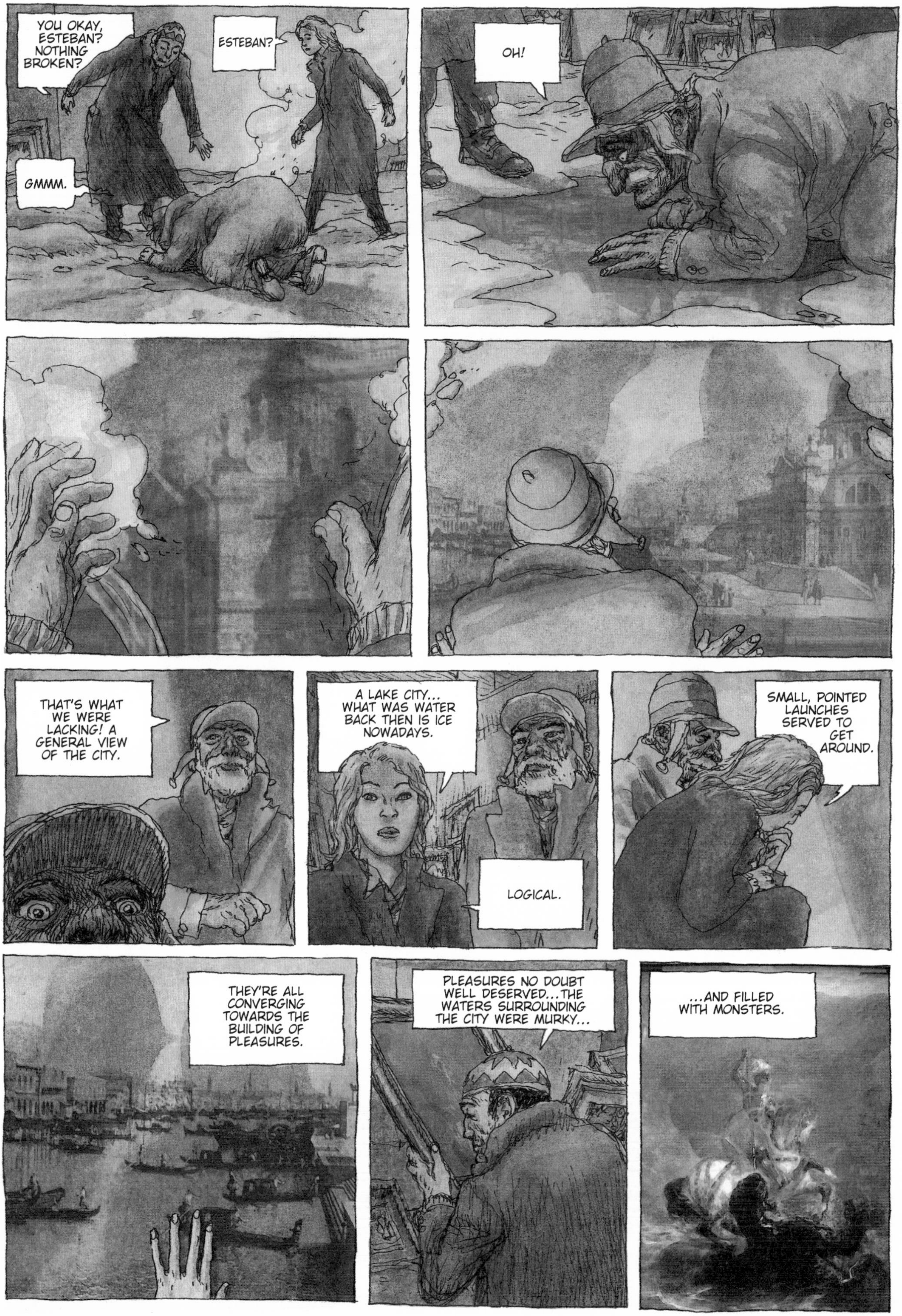
YOU OKAY, ESTEBAN? NOTHING BROKEN?
ESTEBAN?
GMMM.
OH!
THAT'S WHAT WE WERE LACKING! A GENERAL VIEW OF THE CITY.
A LAKE CITY... WHAT WAS WATER BACK THEN IS ICE NOWADAYS.
LOGICAL.
SMALL, POINTED LAUNCHES SERVED TO GET AROUND.
THEY'RE ALL CONVERGING TOWARDS THE BUILDING OF PLEASURES.
PLEASURES NO DOUBT WELL DESERVED... THE WATERS SURROUNDING THE CITY WERE MURKY...
...AND FILLED WITH MONSTERS.

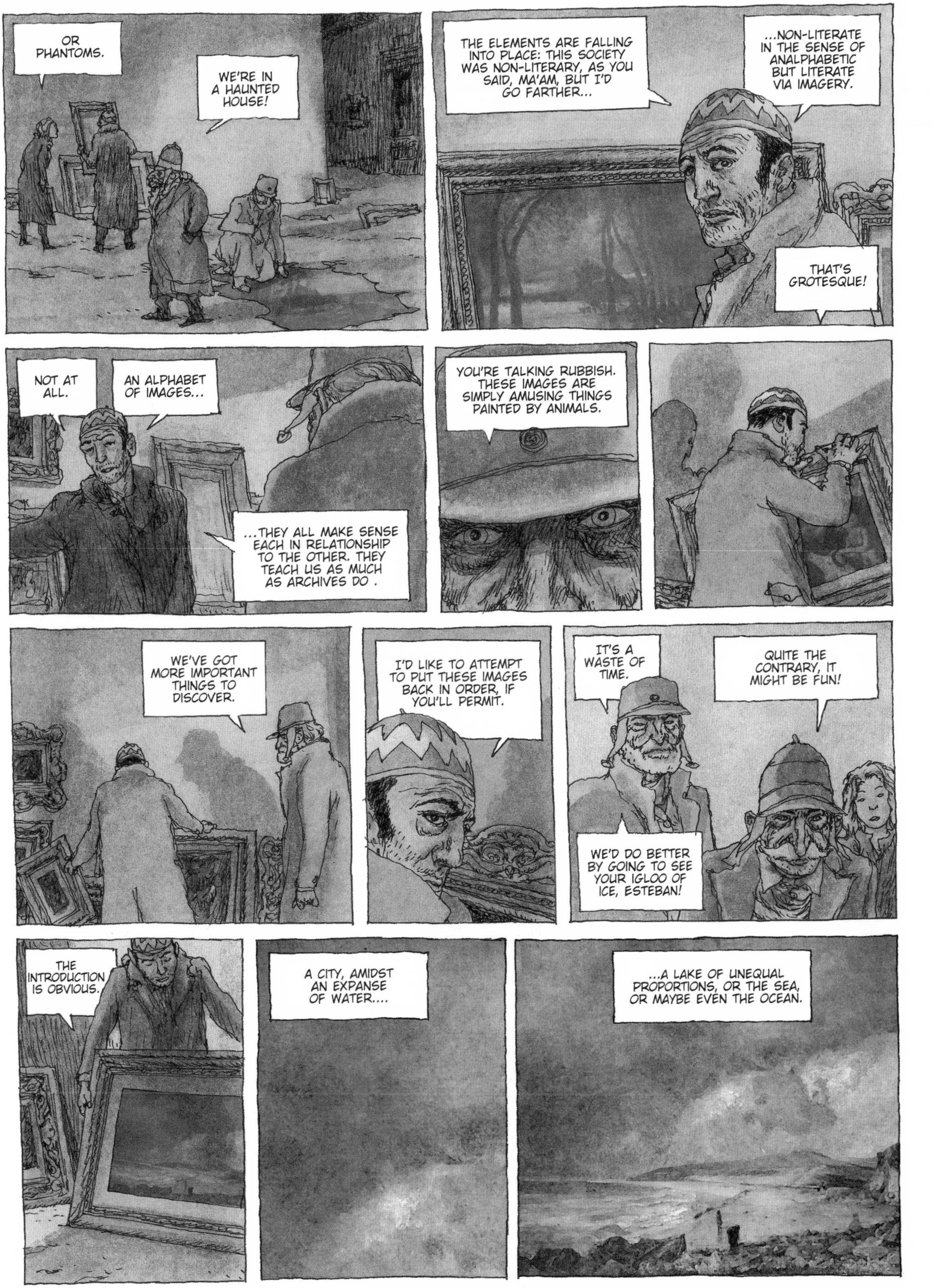
OR PHANTOMS.
WE'RE IN A HAUNTED HOUSE!
THE ELEMENTS ARE FALLING INTO PLACE: THIS SOCIETY WAS NON-LITERARY, AS YOU SAID, MA'AM, BUT I'D GO FARTHER...
...NON-LITERATE IN THE SENSE OF ANALPHABETIC BUT LITERATE VIA IMAGERY.
THAT'S GROTESQUE!
NOT AT ALL.
AN ALPHABET OF IMAGES...
...THEY ALL MAKE SENSE EACH IN RELATIONSHIP TO THE OTHER. THEY TEACH US AS MUCH AS ARCHIVES DO .
YOU'RE TALKING RUBBISH. THESE IMAGES ARE SIMPLY AMUSING THINGS PAINTED BY ANIMALS.
WE'VE GOT MORE IMPORTANT THINGS TO DISCOVER.
I'D LIKE TO ATTEMPT TO PUT THESE IMAGES BACK IN ORDER, IF YOU'LL PERMIT.
IT'S A WASTE OF TIME.
QUITE THE CONTRARY, IT MIGHT BE FUN!
WE'D DO BETTER BY GOING TO SEE YOUR IGLOO OF ICE, ESTEBAN!
THE INTRODUCTION IS OBVIOUS.
A CITY, AMIDST AN EXPANSE OF WATER....
...A LAKE OF UNEQUAL PROPORTIONS, OR THE SEA, OR MAYBE EVEN THE OCEAN.

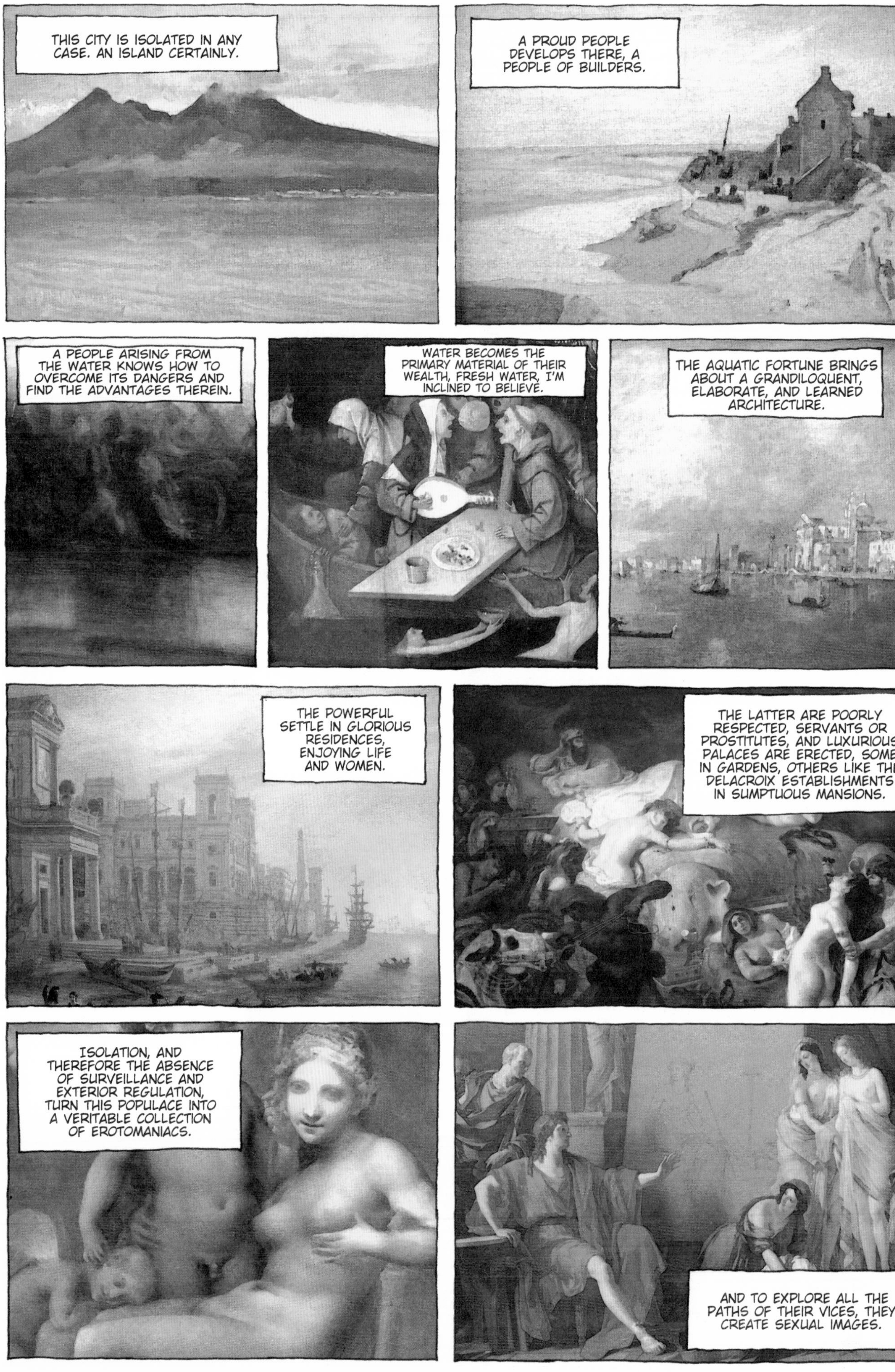
THIS CITY IS ISOLATED IN ANY CASE. AN ISLAND CERTAINLY.
A PROUD PEOPLE DEVELOPS THERE, A PEOPLE OF BUILDERS.
A PEOPLE ARISING FROM THE WATER KNOWS HOW TO OVERCOME ITS DANGERS AND FIND THE ADVANTAGES THEREIN.
WATER BECOMES THE PRIMARY MATERIAL OF THEIR WEALTH, FRESH WATER, I'M INCLINED TO BELIEVE.
THE AQUATIC FORTUNE BRINGS ABOUT A GRANDILOQUENT, ELABORATE, AND LEARNED ARCHITECTURE.
THE POWERFUL SETTLE IN GLORIOUS RESIDENCES, ENJOYING LIFE AND WOMEN.
THE LATTER ARE POORLY RESPECTED, SERVANTS OR PROSTITUTES, AND LUXURIOUS PALACES ARE ERECTED, SOME IN GARDENS, OTHERS LIKE THE DELACROIX ESTABLISHMENTS IN SUMPTUOUS MANSIONS.
ISOLATION, AND THEREFORE THE ABSENCE OF SURVEILLANCE AND EXTERIOR REGULATION, TURN THIS POPULACE INTO A VERITABLE COLLECTION OF EROTOMANIACS.
AND TO EXPLORE ALL THE PATHS OF THEIR VICES, THEY CREATE SEXUAL IMAGES.

YOU DON'T THINK THEY MIGHT, ON THE CONTRARY, HAVE SUFFERED FROM A LACK OF DESIRE, AND THAT THESE IMAGES WERE AN AID FOR PROCREATION?

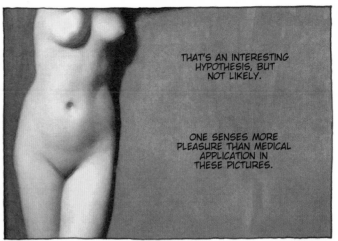

THAT'S AN INTERESTING HYPOTHESIS, BUT NOT LIKELY.

ONE SENSES MORE PLEASURE THAN MEDICAL APPLICATION IN THESE PICTURES.

ANIMALS PARTICIPATE IN HUMAN ACTIVITIES.

MAYBE BECAUSE THEY, TOO, AROSE FROM THE WATER.

BUT THE HIERARCHY OF INTELLIGENCE IS RESPECTED, BACK THEN AS NOWADAYS, AND ANIMALS PLEDGE ALLEGIANCE TO MANKIND.

EVEN IF CERTAIN HUMANS PRESENT SOME PARTICULAR GENETIC FORMS...

...THAT ONE WOULD PRESUME BORROWED FROM THE ANIMAL REALM. A FORETASTE OF WHAT WE KNOW TODAY. BUT THE ABERRATIONS SEEM RATHER RARE...

...EXCEPTING THOSE OBESE, FLYING CHILDREN, AN IMPROBABLE PHENOMENON FOR WHICH WE MUST FIND A CREDIBLE EXPLANATION.

LEVITATION ISN'T RESERVED SOLELY TO THE NEWBORN, IT SEEMS.

INDEED: A PORTION OF THE POPULACE LEVITATES...MAYBE AS AN EFFECT OF BEING CONSUMED.

A SPECIAL PROPELLING ENERGY, UNKNOWN TO US, A SORT OF ENERGY-PRODUCING PUTREFACTION.

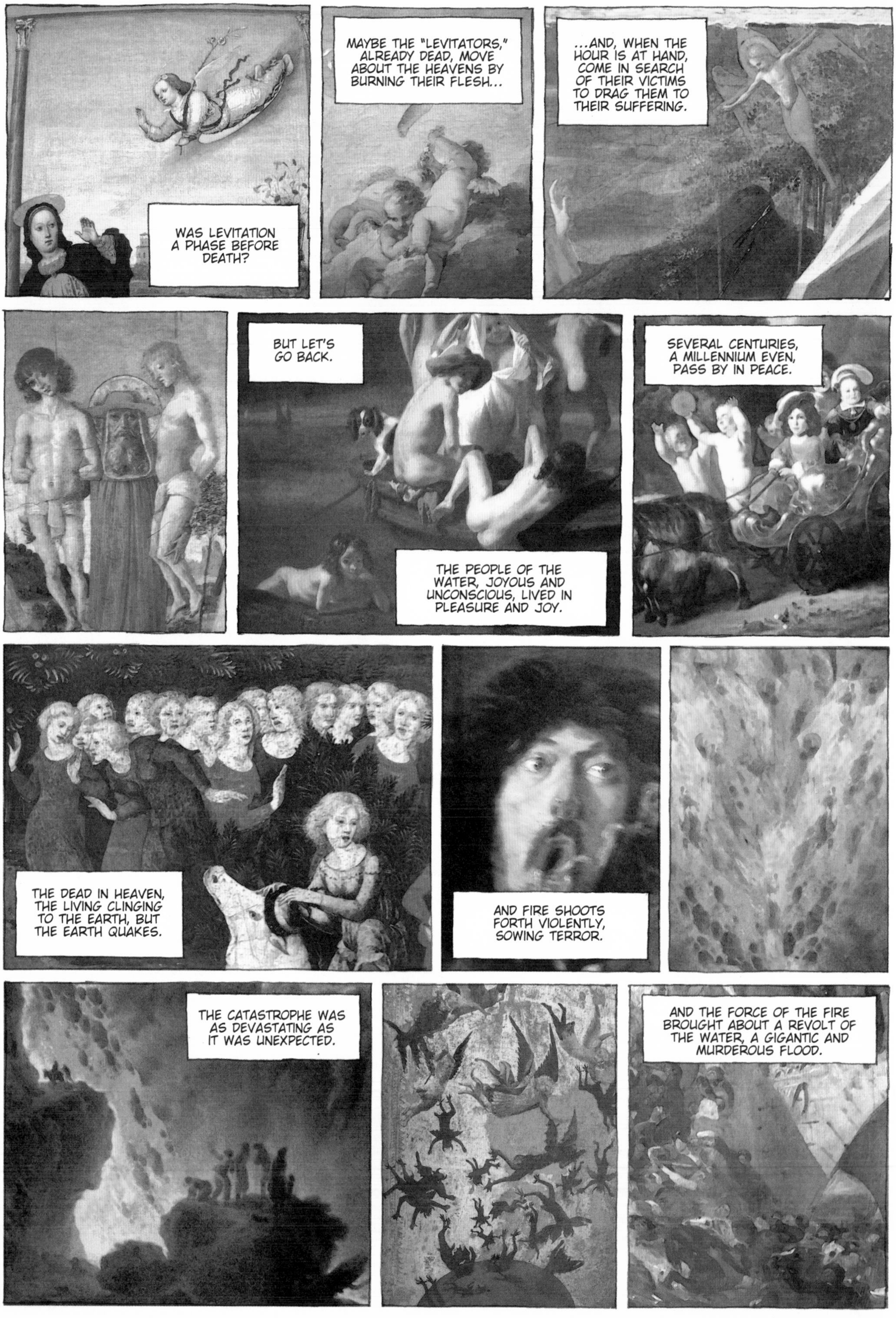
WAS LEVITATION A PHASE BEFORE DEATH?
MAYBE THE "LEVITATORS," ALREADY DEAD, MOVE ABOUT THE HEAVENS BY BURNING THEIR FLESH...
...AND, WHEN THE HOUR IS AT HAND, COME IN SEARCH OF THEIR VICTIMS TO DRAG THEM TO THEIR SUFFERING.
BUT LET'S GO BACK.
THE PEOPLE OF THE WATER, JOYOUS AND UNCONSCIOUS, LIVED IN PLEASURE AND JOY.
SEVERAL CENTURIES, A MILLENNIUM EVEN, PASS BY IN PEACE.
THE DEAD IN HEAVEN, THE LIVING CLINGING TO THE EARTH, BUT THE EARTH QUAKES.
AND FIRE SHOOTS FORTH VIOLENTLY, SOWING TERROR.
THE CATASTROPHE WAS AS DEVASTATING AS IT WAS UNEXPECTED.
AND THE FORCE OF THE FIRE BROUGHT ABOUT A REVOLT OF THE WATER, A GIGANTIC AND MURDEROUS FLOOD.

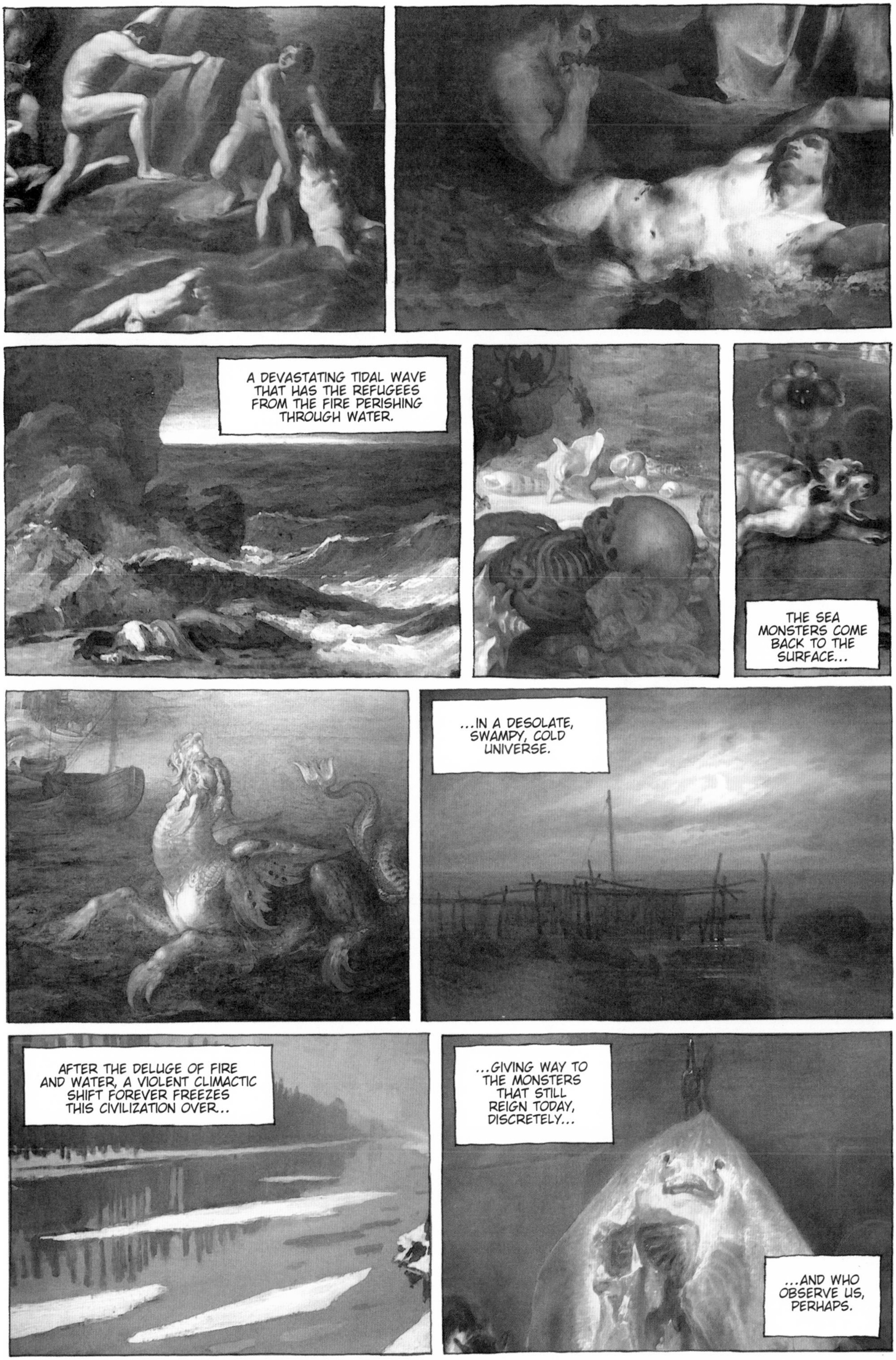
A DEVASTATING TIDAL WAVE THAT HAS THE REFUGEES FROM THE FIRE PERISHING THROUGH WATER.
THE SEA MONSTERS COME BACK TO THE SURFACE...
...IN A DESOLATE, SWAMPY, COLD UNIVERSE.
AFTER THE DELUGE OF FIRE AND WATER, A VIOLENT CLIMACTIC SHIFT FOREVER FREEZES THIS CIVILIZATION OVER...
...GIVING WAY TO THE MONSTERS THAT STILL REIGN TODAY, DISCRETELY...
...AND WHO OBSERVE US, PERHAPS.

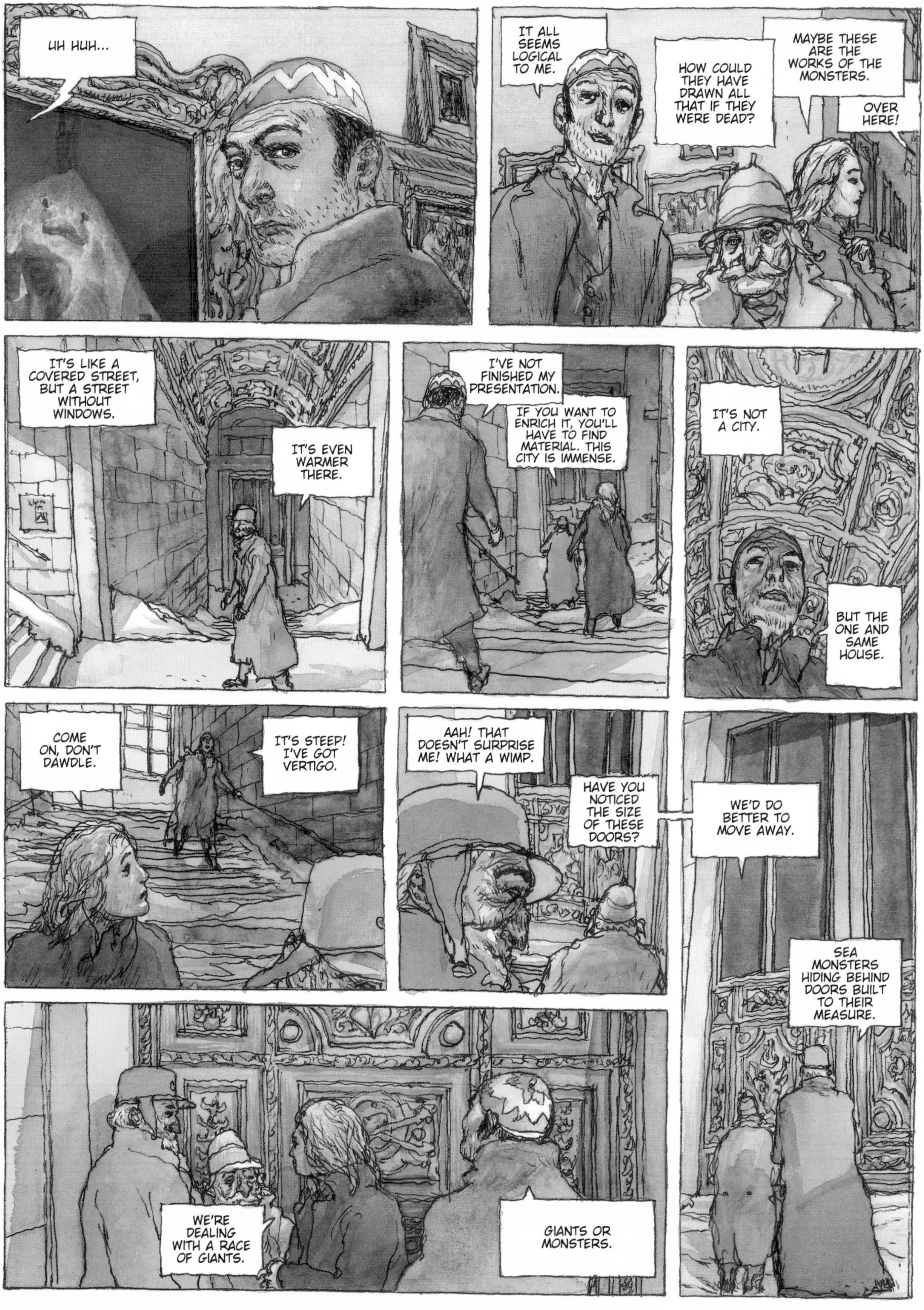
UH HUH...
IT ALL SEEMS LOGICAL TO ME.
HOW COULD THEY HAVE DRAWN ALL THAT IF THEY WERE DEAD?
MAYBE THESE ARE THE WORKS OF THE MONSTERS.
OVER HERE!
IT'S LIKE A COVERED STREET, BUT A STREET WITHOUT WINDOWS.
IT'S EVEN WARMER THERE.
I'VE NOT FINISHED MY PRESENTATION.
IF YOU WANT TO ENRICH IT, YOU'LL HAVE TO FIND MATERIAL. THIS CITY IS IMMENSE.
IT'S NOT A CITY.
BUT THE ONE AND SAME HOUSE.
COME ON, DON'T DAWDLE.
IT'S STEEP! I'VE GOT VERTIGO.
AAH! THAT DOESN'T SURPRISE ME! WHAT A WIMP.
HAVE YOU NOTICED THE SIZE OF THESE DOORS?
WE'D DO BETTER TO MOVE AWAY.
SEA MONSTERS HIDING BEHIND DOORS BUILT TO THEIR MEASURE.
WE'RE DEALING WITH A RACE OF GIANTS.
GIANTS OR MONSTERS.

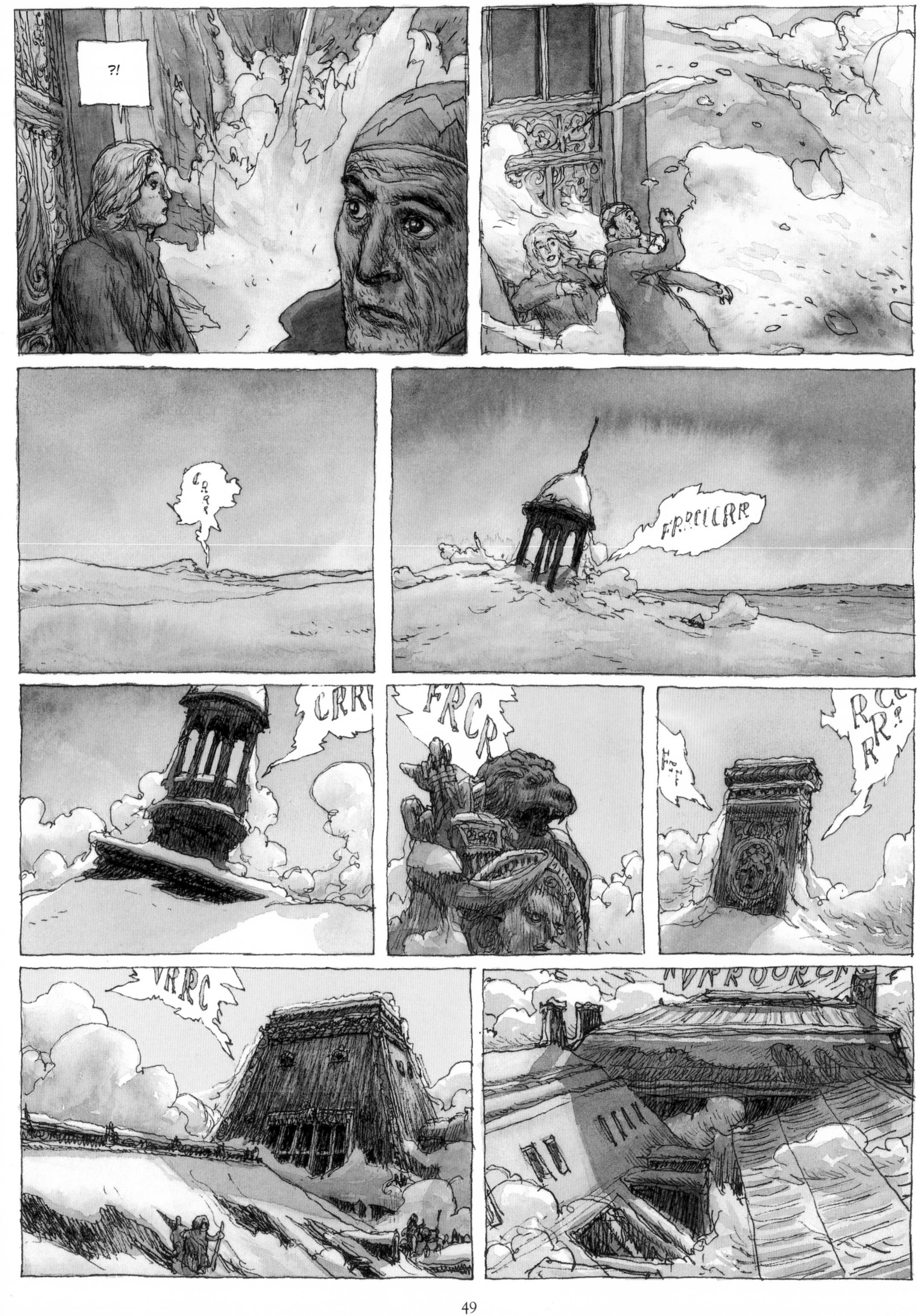
?!
FRRCCCRR
CRR
FRCR
VRRC

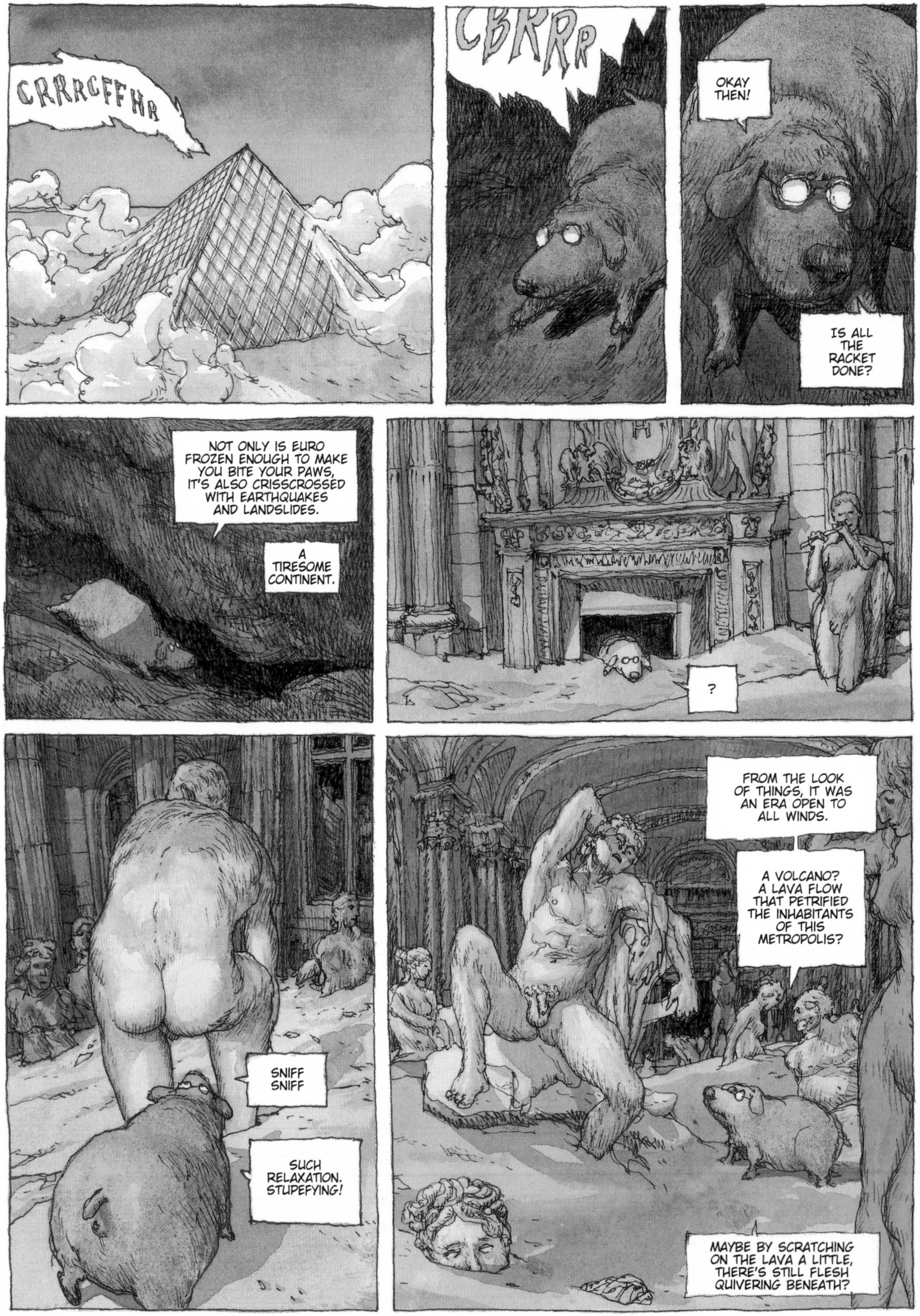
CRRRCFFHR
CBRRR
OKAY THEN!
IS ALL THE RACKET DONE?
NOT ONLY IS EURO FROZEN ENOUGH TO MAKE YOU BITE YOUR PAWS, IT'S ALSO CRISSCROSSED WITH EARTHQUAKES AND LANDSLIDES.
A TIRESOME CONTINENT.
?
SNIFF SNIFF
SUCH RELAXATION. STUPEFYING!
FROM THE LOOK OF THINGS, IT WAS AN ERA OPEN TO ALL WINDS.
A VOLCANO? A LAVA FLOW THAT PETRIFIED THE INHABITANTS OF THIS METROPOLIS?
MAYBE BY SCRATCHING ON THE LAVA A LITTLE, THERE'S STILL FLESH QUIVERING BENEATH?

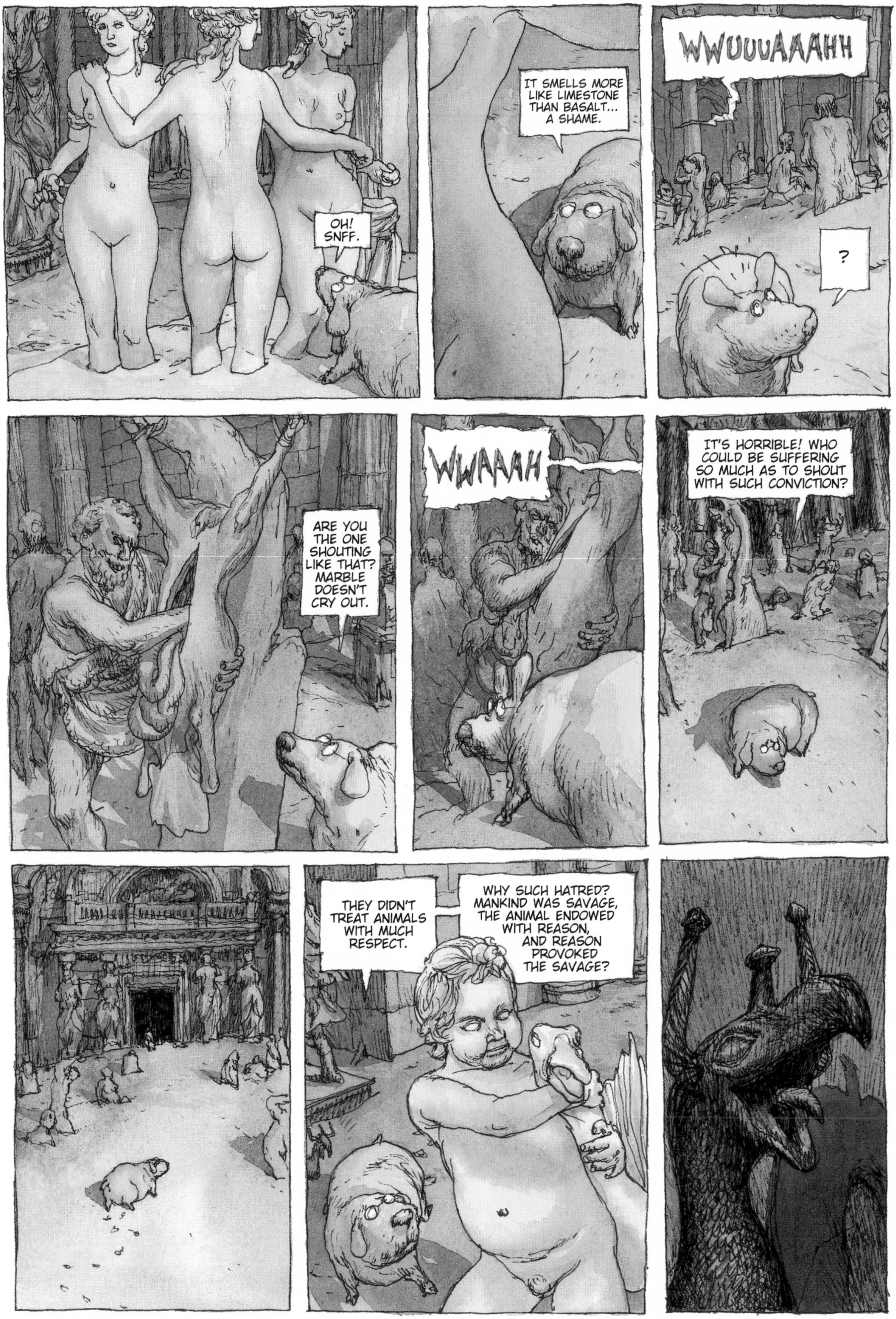
OH! SNFF.
IT SMELLS MORE LIKE LIMESTONE THAN BASALT... A SHAME.
WWUUUAAAHH
?
ARE YOU THE ONE SHOUTING LIKE THAT? MARBLE DOESN'T CRY OUT.
WWAAAH
IT'S HORRIBLE! WHO COULD BE SUFFERING SO MUCH AS TO SHOUT WITH SUCH CONVICTION?
THEY DIDN'T TREAT ANIMALS WITH MUCH RESPECT.
WHY SUCH HATRED? MANKIND WAS SAVAGE, THE ANIMAL ENDOWED WITH REASON, AND REASON PROVOKED THE SAVAGE?

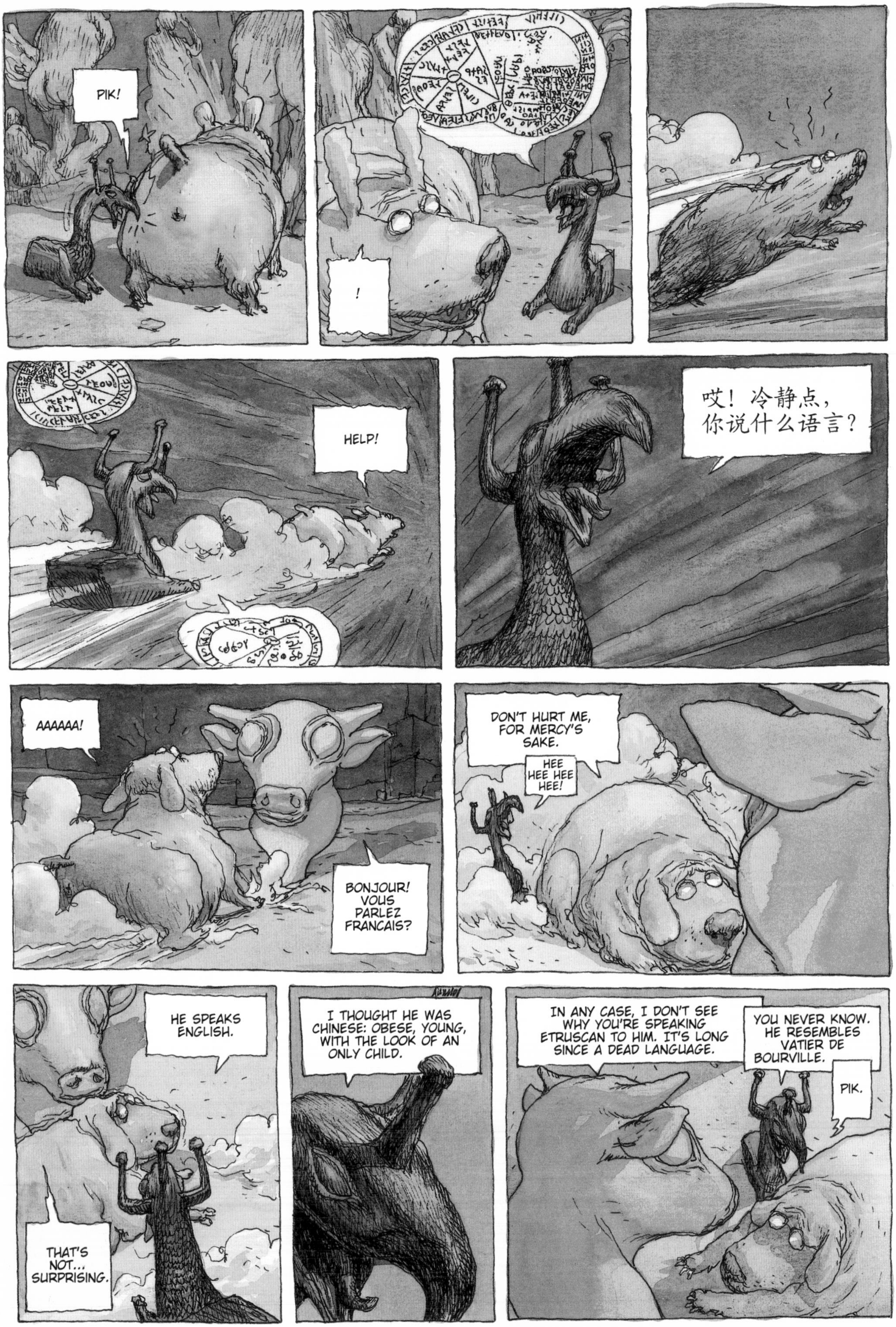
PIK!
!
HELP!
哎！冷静点，
你说什么语言？
AAAAAA!
BONJOUR! VOUS PARLEZ FRANCAIS?
DON'T HURT ME, FOR MERCY'S SAKE.
HEE HEE HEE HEE!
HE SPEAKS ENGLISH.
THAT'S NOT... SURPRISING.
I THOUGHT HE WAS CHINESE: OBESE, YOUNG, WITH THE LOOK OF AN ONLY CHILD.
IN ANY CASE, I DON'T SEE WHY YOU'RE SPEAKING ETRUSCAN TO HIM. IT'S LONG SINCE A DEAD LANGUAGE.
YOU NEVER KNOW. HE RESEMBLES VATIER DE BOURVILLE.
PIK.

IT'S TRUE HE HAS A RESEMBLANCE TO VATIER DE BOURVILLE. IT'S ASTONISHING.

HEY! VATIER!! LOOK AT THIS!

LEAVE ME THE HELL ALONE.

WHAT A CUR.

HE HASN'T BEEN OUT OF HIS DISPLAY CASE IN CENTURIES: HE'S BASTING IN HIS JUICES.

BORN ETRUSCAN, HE REMAINS ETRUSCAN, AND HE'LL DIE ETRUSCAN.

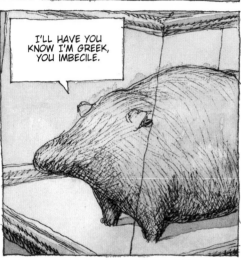

I'LL HAVE YOU KNOW I'M GREEK, YOU IMBECILE.

WHATEVER! FOISTING HIMSELF OFF AS GREEK LIKE THAT. I DON'T SEE HOW IT GETS HIM ANYWHERE.

YOU'RE NOT A GREEK, EITHER, WHILE WE'RE AT IT?

A WHAT?

PIK

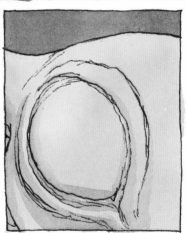

TELL ME, MY FRIEND, WHERE DID YOU COME FROM?

I'M FROM THE SOUTH.

WIIARK!

THAT'S HORRIBLE.

IT'S HARMENSZ AGAIN.

HE'S A COLLEAGUE OF MINE.

..A STEER.

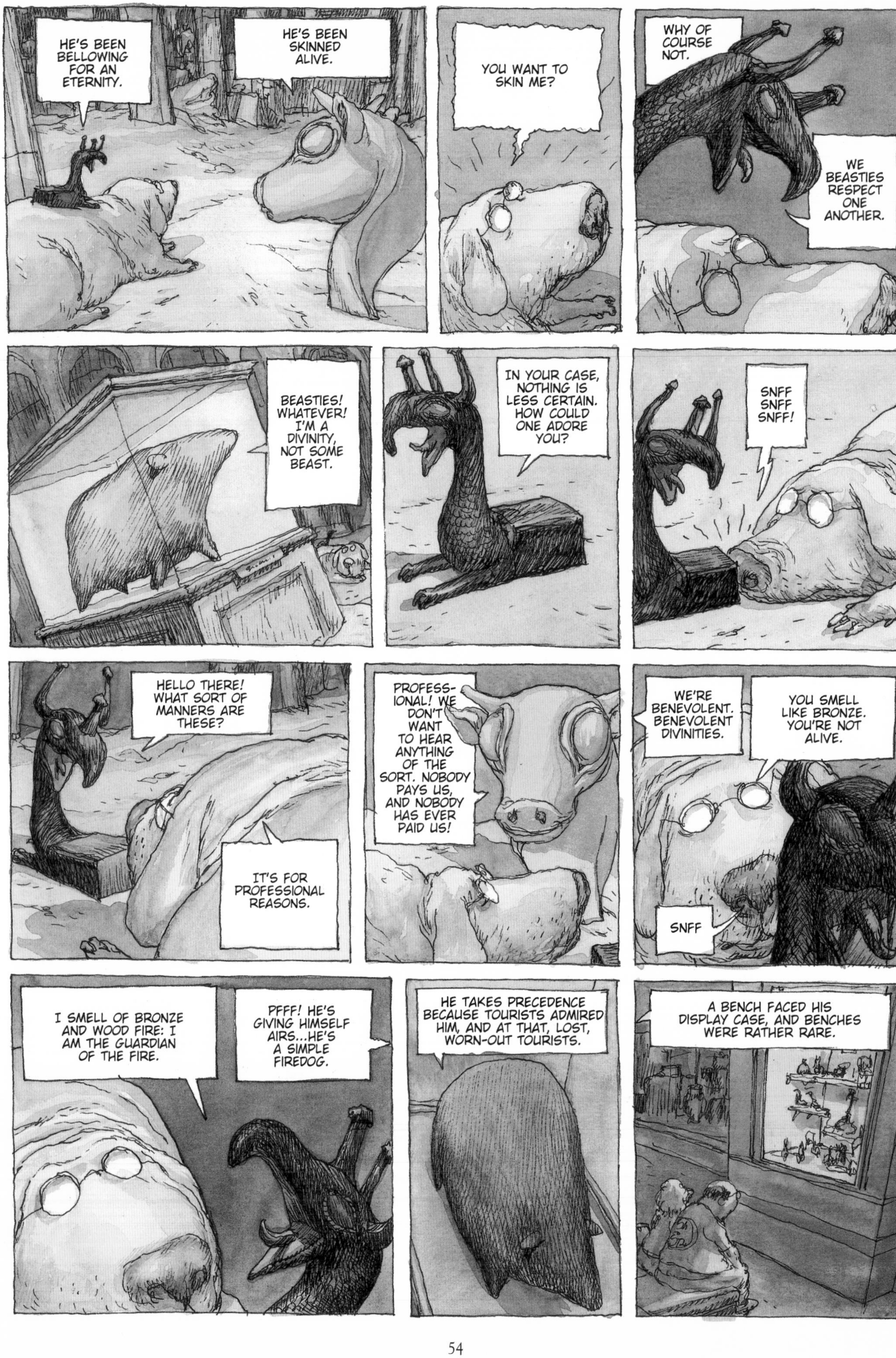
HE'S BEEN BELLOWING FOR AN ETERNITY.
HE'S BEEN SKINNED ALIVE.
YOU WANT TO SKIN ME?
WHY OF COURSE NOT.
WE BEASTIES RESPECT ONE ANOTHER.
BEASTIES! WHATEVER! I'M A DIVINITY, NOT SOME BEAST.
IN YOUR CASE, NOTHING IS LESS CERTAIN. HOW COULD ONE ADORE YOU?
SNFF SNFF SNFF!
HELLO THERE! WHAT SORT OF MANNERS ARE THESE?
IT'S FOR PROFESSIONAL REASONS.
PROFESS-IONAL! WE DON'T WANT TO HEAR ANYTHING OF THE SORT. NOBODY PAYS US, AND NOBODY HAS EVER PAID US!
WE'RE BENEVOLENT. BENEVOLENT DIVINITIES.
YOU SMELL LIKE BRONZE. YOU'RE NOT ALIVE.
SNFF
I SMELL OF BRONZE AND WOOD FIRE: I AM THE GUARDIAN OF THE FIRE.
PFFF! HE'S GIVING HIMSELF AIRS...HE'S A SIMPLE FIREDOG.
HE TAKES PRECEDENCE BECAUSE TOURISTS ADMIRED HIM, AND AT THAT, LOST, WORN-OUT TOURISTS.
A BENCH FACED HIS DISPLAY CASE, AND BENCHES WERE RATHER RARE.

THERE HE WAS, THE POOR THING, A TINY GRIFFON, JUST BEGGING FOR A GLANCE, WHILE ALL AROUND HIM THERE WAS SUCH BETTER STUFF TO SEE.

I AM THE MASTER OF FIRE.

YOU'RE JEALOUS, VATIER.

BECAUSE YOU'RE SO BEAT UP THAT EVERY-ONE MADE FUN OF YOU AND IN EVERY LANGUAGE, TOO!

PFFF!

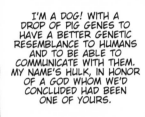

PIG
CYRENAIC - ACQUISITION FROM VATIER DE BOURVILLE 1851

STOP YOUR SQUABBLING. FOR THIS ONCE WE HAVE A VISITOR.

THAT'S RIGHT. MY GOOD PIG, TELL US YOUR INTENTIONS.

I'M NOT A PIG.

I'M A DOG! WITH A DROP OF PIG GENES TO HAVE A BETTER GENETIC RESEMBLANCE TO HUMANS AND TO BE ABLE TO COMMUNICATE WITH THEM. MY NAME'S HULK, IN HONOR OF A GOD WHOM WE'D CONCLUDED HAD BEEN ONE OF YOURS.

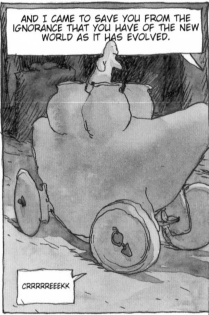

AND I CAME TO SAVE YOU FROM THE IGNORANCE THAT YOU HAVE OF THE NEW WORLD AS IT HAS EVOLVED.

CRRRRREEEKK

HOW'S THAT?

YOU'VE BEEN STUCK IN YOUR FROZEN EURO. YOU DON'T KNOW ANYTHING.

WELL THEN!

HE'S A PRETENTIOUS ONE!

THE YOUNGER THEY ARE, THE MORE PRETENTIOUS!

HE'S YOUNG, BUT HE HAS THE ADVANTAGE OF BEING OF FLESH AND BLOOD, AND OF HAVING A LITTLE, BEATING HEART.

SNFF

HE DOESN'T HAVE A SAVIOR'S PHYSIQUE, BUT LET'S REMEMBER THAT CLOTHES DON'T MAKE THE MAN.

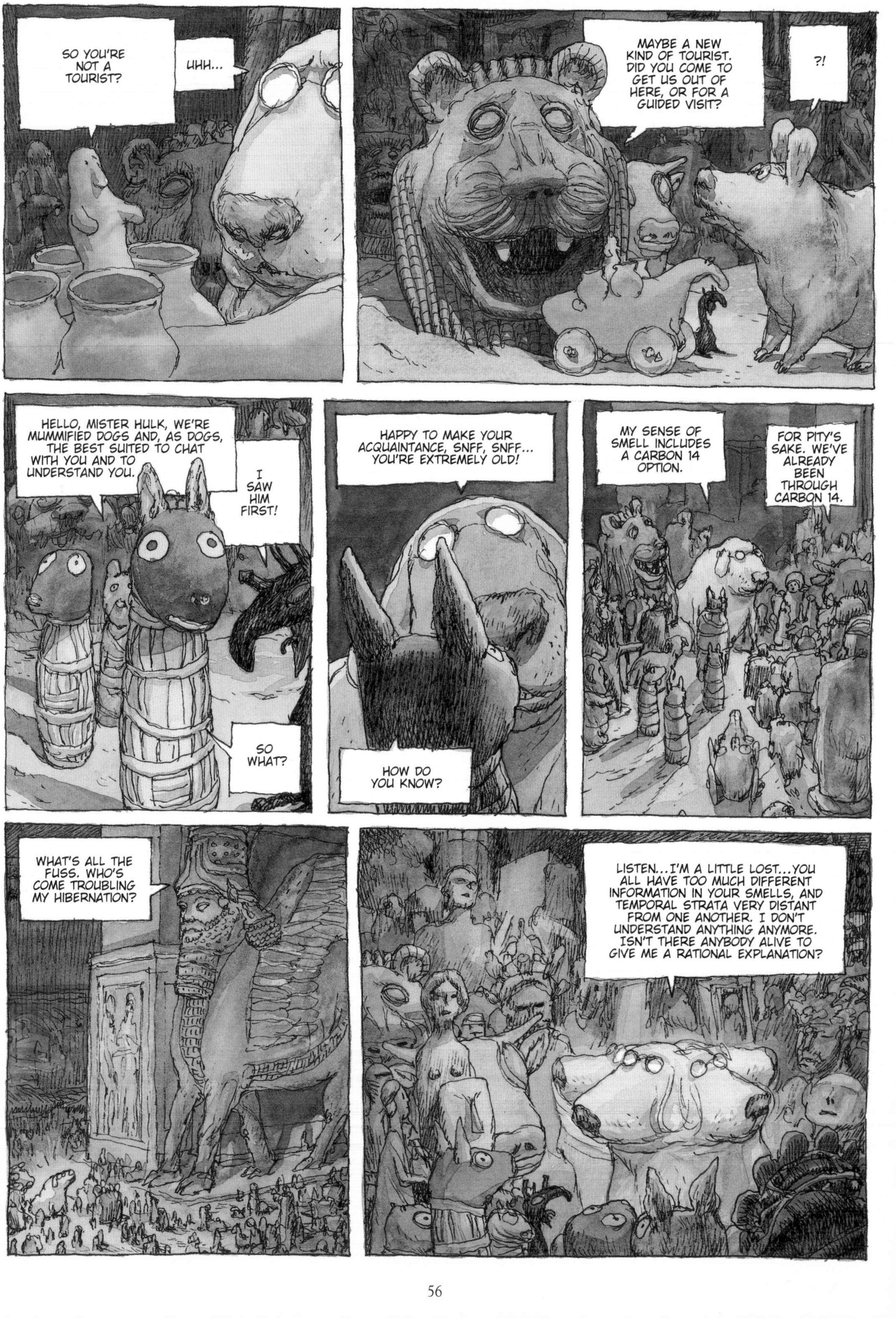

SO YOU'RE NOT A TOURIST?
UHH...
MAYBE A NEW KIND OF TOURIST. DID YOU COME TO GET US OUT OF HERE, OR FOR A GUIDED VISIT?
?!
HELLO, MISTER HULK, WE'RE MUMMIFIED DOGS AND, AS DOGS, THE BEST SUITED TO CHAT WITH YOU AND TO UNDERSTAND YOU.
I SAW HIM FIRST!
SO WHAT?
HAPPY TO MAKE YOUR ACQUAINTANCE, SNFF, SNFF... YOU'RE EXTREMELY OLD!
HOW DO YOU KNOW?
MY SENSE OF SMELL INCLUDES A CARBON 14 OPTION.
FOR PITY'S SAKE. WE'VE ALREADY BEEN THROUGH CARBON 14.
WHAT'S ALL THE FUSS. WHO'S COME TROUBLING MY HIBERNATION?
LISTEN...I'M A LITTLE LOST...YOU ALL HAVE TOO MUCH DIFFERENT INFORMATION IN YOUR SMELLS, AND TEMPORAL STRATA VERY DISTANT FROM ONE ANOTHER. I DON'T UNDERSTAND ANYTHING ANYMORE. ISN'T THERE ANYBODY ALIVE TO GIVE ME A RATIONAL EXPLANATION?

YES, ME! I'M FILLED WITH THE ASHES OF A BODY THAT ONCE LIVED. I'M FILLED WITH ITS EXISTENCE.

ME, TOO, AND I HAVE EVEN MORE! MY LIFE WAS PASSIONATE.

NO, NOT ASHES. I WANT TO SENSE A BEATING HEART.

IF WE MUST SPEAK OF BEING ALIVE, THEN I'M THE ONE YOU WANT.

WE'RE JUST LIKE SEA-SHELLS.

THE BEST STUFF'S INSIDE.

YOU'RE NOT VERY FRESH ANYMORE.

I'M FRESH IN THE MEMORY OF MEN.

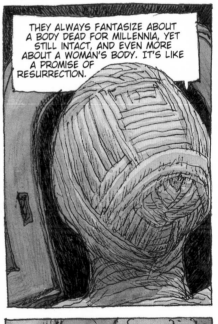

THEY ALWAYS FANTASIZE ABOUT A BODY DEAD FOR MILLENNIA, YET STILL INTACT, AND EVEN MORE ABOUT A WOMAN'S BODY. IT'S LIKE A PROMISE OF RESURRECTION.

I'M NOT CONVINCED.

THERE'S ALSO C.D.D., BUT HIS HEART'S NO LONGER BEATING.

C.D.D.?

HE'S THE YOUNGEST ONE HERE...OUR STENDHAL SYNDROME. THE ONLY WORK FROM AFTER 1948 TO HAVE REMAINED ON SITE.

?

WE CONSIDER HIM A WORK OF ART, FOR THE COLD FROZE HIM IN THE POSTURE OF A SINCERE ART LOVER.

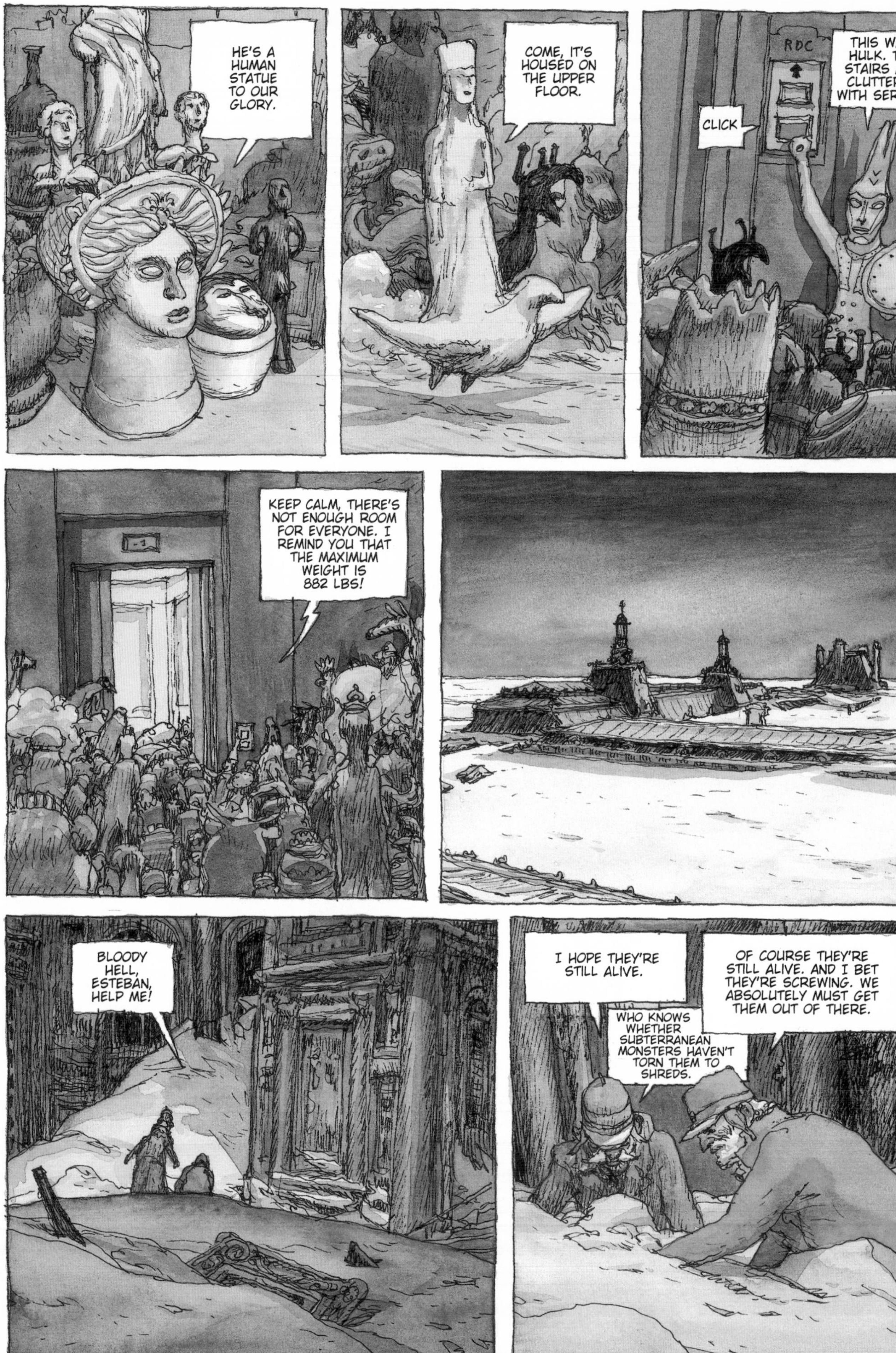
HE'S A HUMAN STATUE TO OUR GLORY.
COME, IT'S HOUSED ON THE UPPER FLOOR.
RDC
CLICK
THIS WAY, HULK. THE STAIRS ARE CLUTTERED WITH SERACS.
KEEP CALM, THERE'S NOT ENOUGH ROOM FOR EVERYONE. I REMIND YOU THAT THE MAXIMUM WEIGHT IS 882 LBS!
BLOODY HELL, ESTEBAN, HELP ME!
I HOPE THEY'RE STILL ALIVE.
WHO KNOWS WHETHER SUBTERRANEAN MONSTERS HAVEN'T TORN THEM TO SHREDS.
OF COURSE THEY'RE STILL ALIVE. AND I BET THEY'RE SCREWING. WE ABSOLUTELY MUST GET THEM OUT OF THERE.

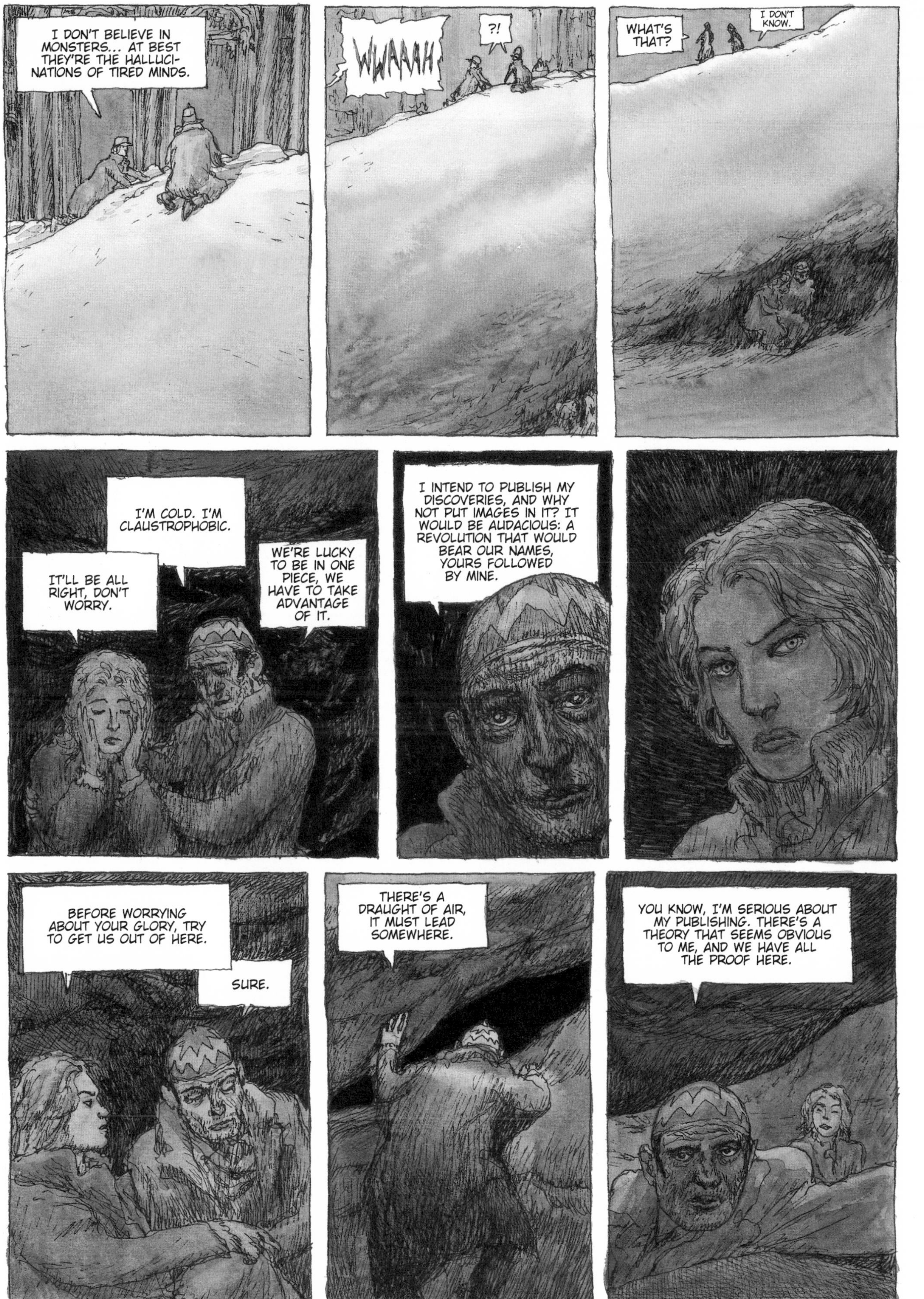
I DON'T BELIEVE IN MONSTERS... AT BEST THEY'RE THE HALLUCINATIONS OF TIRED MINDS.
WWAAAH
?!
WHAT'S THAT?
I DON'T KNOW.
I'M COLD. I'M CLAUSTROPHOBIC.
IT'LL BE ALL RIGHT, DON'T WORRY.
WE'RE LUCKY TO BE IN ONE PIECE, WE HAVE TO TAKE ADVANTAGE OF IT.
I INTEND TO PUBLISH MY DISCOVERIES, AND WHY NOT PUT IMAGES IN IT? IT WOULD BE AUDACIOUS: A REVOLUTION THAT WOULD BEAR OUR NAMES, YOURS FOLLOWED BY MINE.
BEFORE WORRYING ABOUT YOUR GLORY, TRY TO GET US OUT OF HERE.
SURE.
THERE'S A DRAUGHT OF AIR, IT MUST LEAD SOMEWHERE.
YOU KNOW, I'M SERIOUS ABOUT MY PUBLISHING. THERE'S A THEORY THAT SEEMS OBVIOUS TO ME, AND WE HAVE ALL THE PROOF HERE.

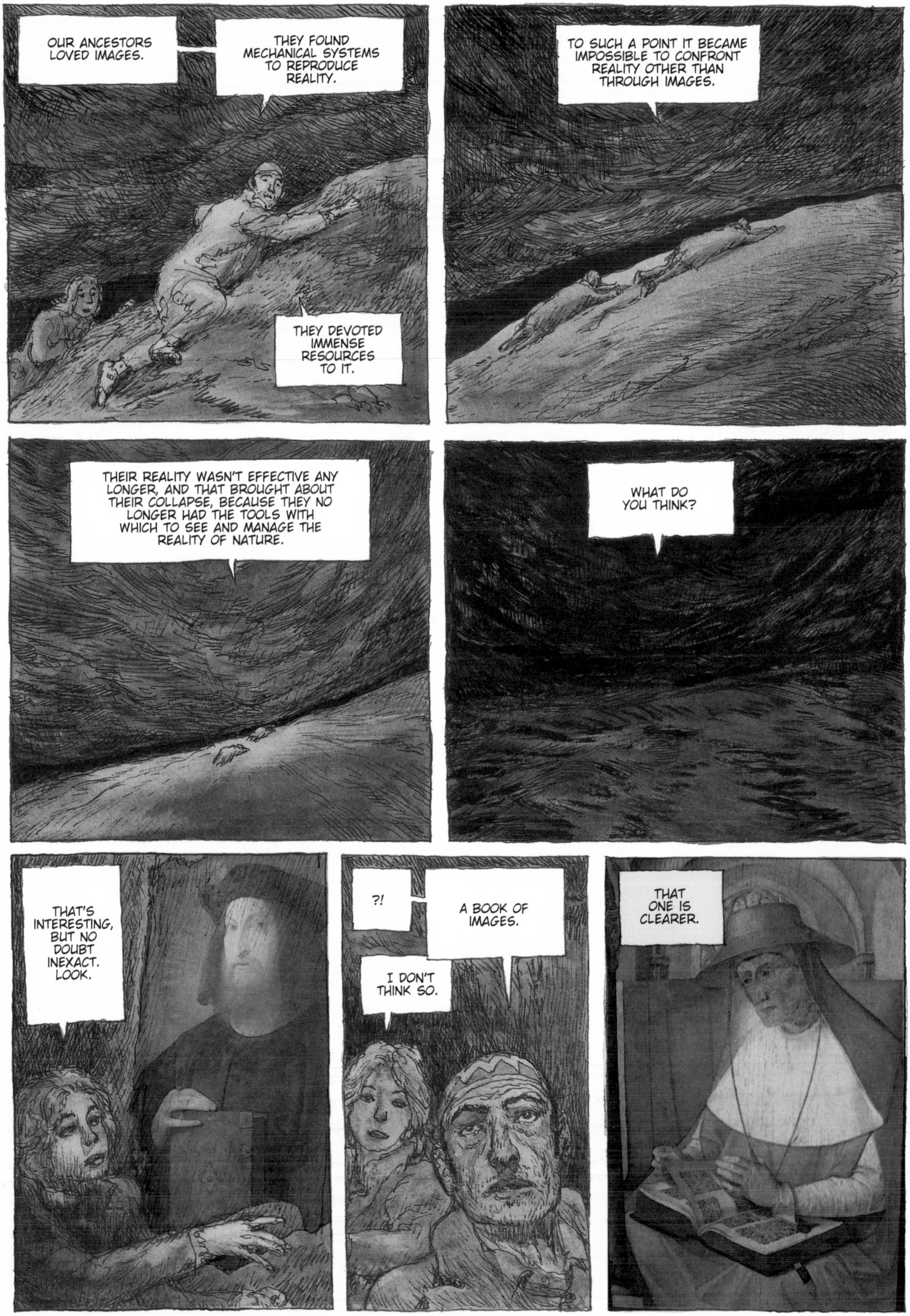
OUR ANCESTORS LOVED IMAGES.
THEY FOUND MECHANICAL SYSTEMS TO REPRODUCE REALITY.
THEY DEVOTED IMMENSE RESOURCES TO IT.
TO SUCH A POINT IT BECAME IMPOSSIBLE TO CONFRONT REALITY OTHER THAN THROUGH IMAGES.
THEIR REALITY WASN'T EFFECTIVE ANY LONGER, AND THAT BROUGHT ABOUT THEIR COLLAPSE, BECAUSE THEY NO LONGER HAD THE TOOLS WITH WHICH TO SEE AND MANAGE THE REALITY OF NATURE.
WHAT DO YOU THINK?
THAT'S INTERESTING, BUT NO DOUBT INEXACT. LOOK.
?!
A BOOK OF IMAGES.
I DON'T THINK SO.
THAT ONE IS CLEARER.

HMMM...

THAT DOESN'T CHANGE ANYTHING.

A FRINGE OF THE POPULATION UNDERSTOOD HOW TO DEVELOP A REALITY THROUGH WORDS; IT'S THE BEGINNINGS OF OUR LANGUAGE.

PERHAPS EVEN THE SUPPORTERS OF IMAGES AND THE SUPPORTERS OF WORDS FOUGHT A WAR WITH ONE ANOTHER.

YOU HAVE AN ANSWER FOR EVERYTHING. YOUR STORIES FLUCTUATE.

YOU LACK SCIENTIFIC RIGOR. I'M NOT SURE YOUR FUTURE PUBLICATIONS WILL BE CONVINCING.

YOU'RE DRAGGING US INTO THE OBSCURITY OF YOUR IMAGINATION.

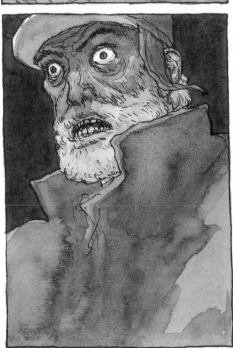

WAAIII

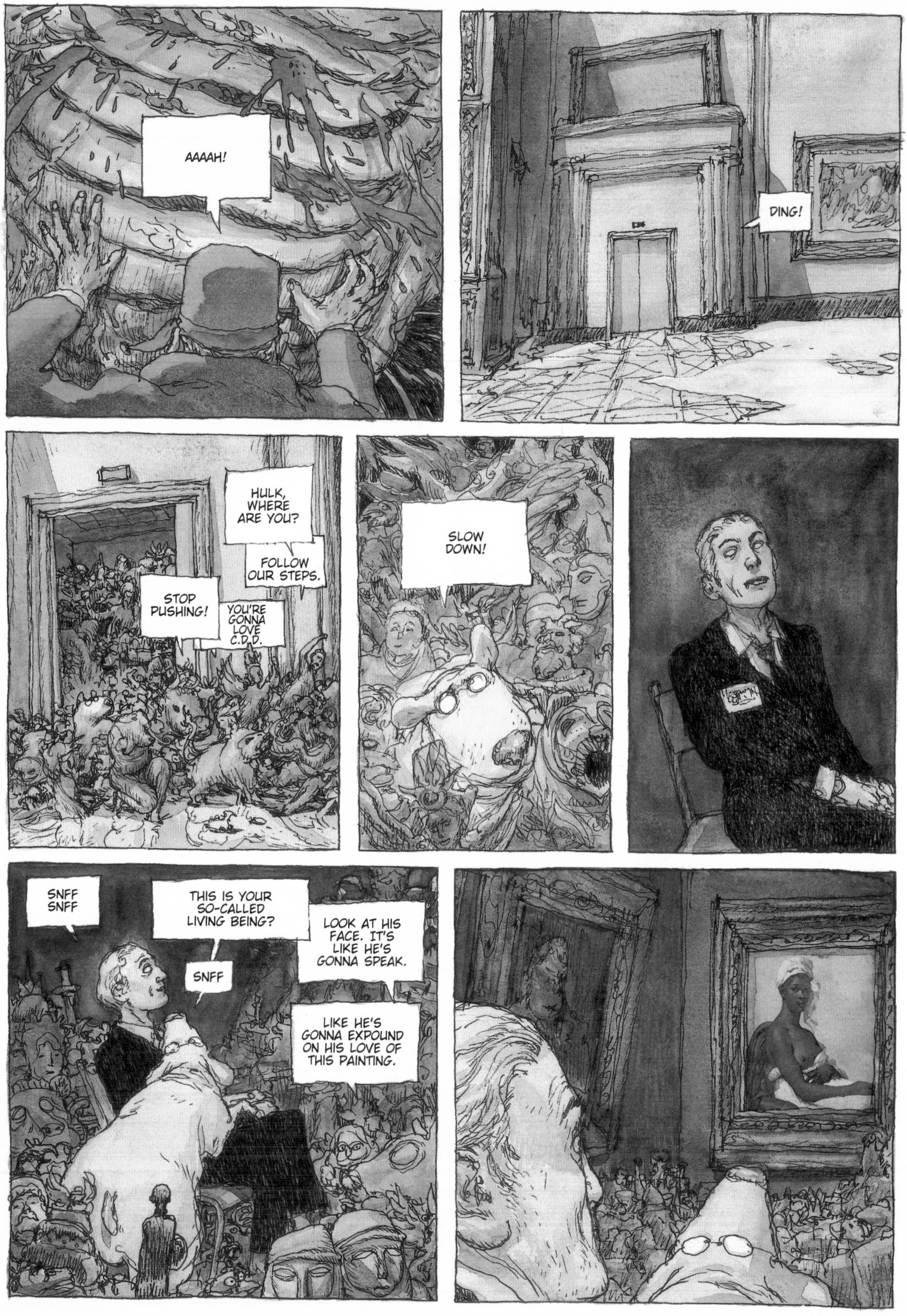
AAAAH!
DING!
HULK, WHERE ARE YOU?
FOLLOW OUR STEPS.
STOP PUSHING!
YOU'RE GONNA LOVE C.D.D.
SLOW DOWN!
SNFF SNFF
THIS IS YOUR SO-CALLED LIVING BEING?
SNFF
LOOK AT HIS FACE. IT'S LIKE HE'S GONNA SPEAK.
LIKE HE'S GONNA EXPOUND ON HIS LOVE OF THIS PAINTING.

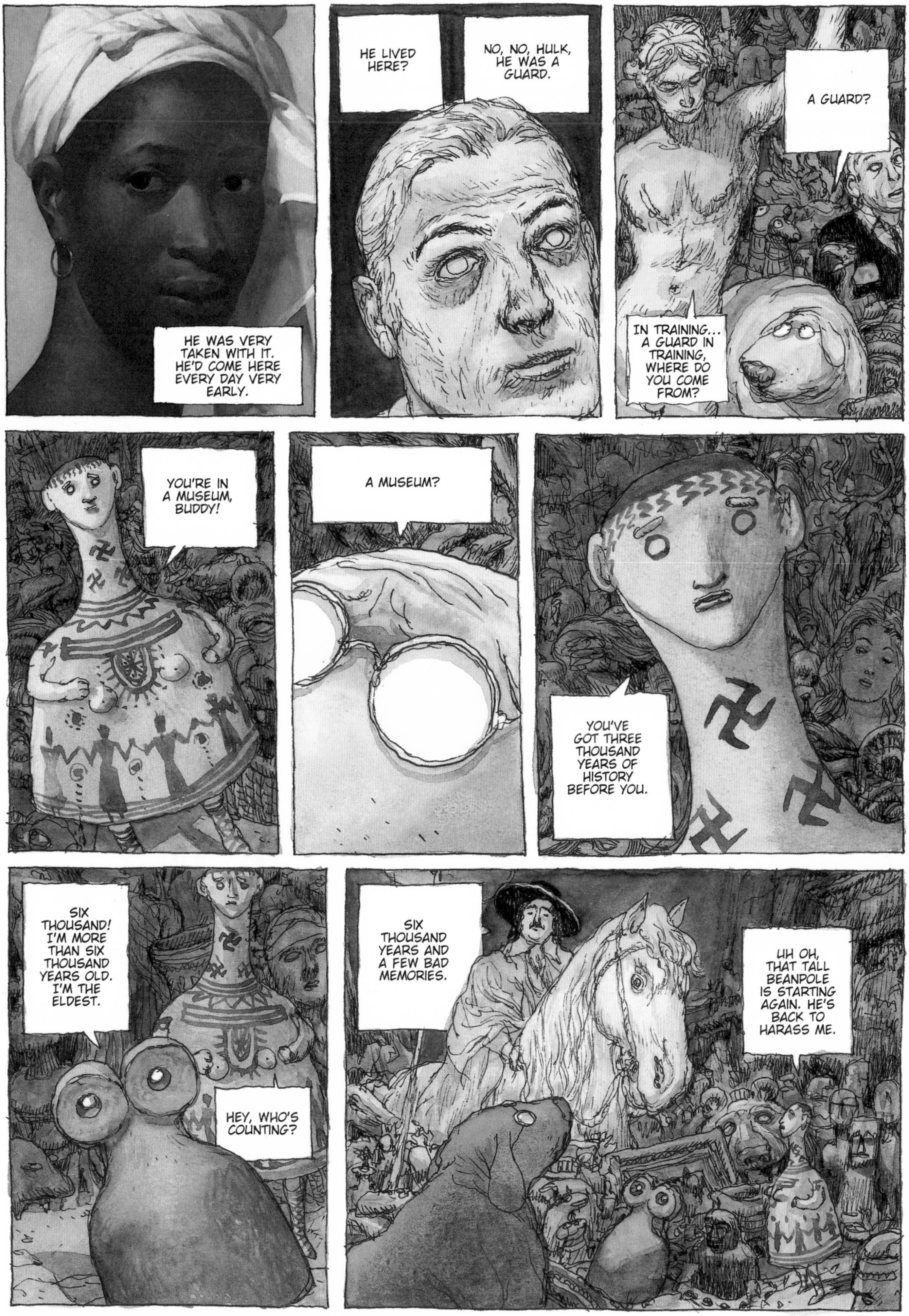
HE WAS VERY TAKEN WITH IT. HE'D COME HERE EVERY DAY VERY EARLY.
HE LIVED HERE?
NO, NO, HULK, HE WAS A GUARD.
A GUARD?
IN TRAINING... A GUARD IN TRAINING, WHERE DO YOU COME FROM?
YOU'RE IN A MUSEUM, BUDDY!
A MUSEUM?
YOU'VE GOT THREE THOUSAND YEARS OF HISTORY BEFORE YOU.
SIX THOUSAND! I'M MORE THAN SIX THOUSAND YEARS OLD. I'M THE ELDEST.
HEY, WHO'S COUNTING?
SIX THOUSAND YEARS AND A FEW BAD MEMORIES.
UH OH, THAT TALL BEANPOLE IS STARTING AGAIN. HE'S BACK TO HARASS ME.

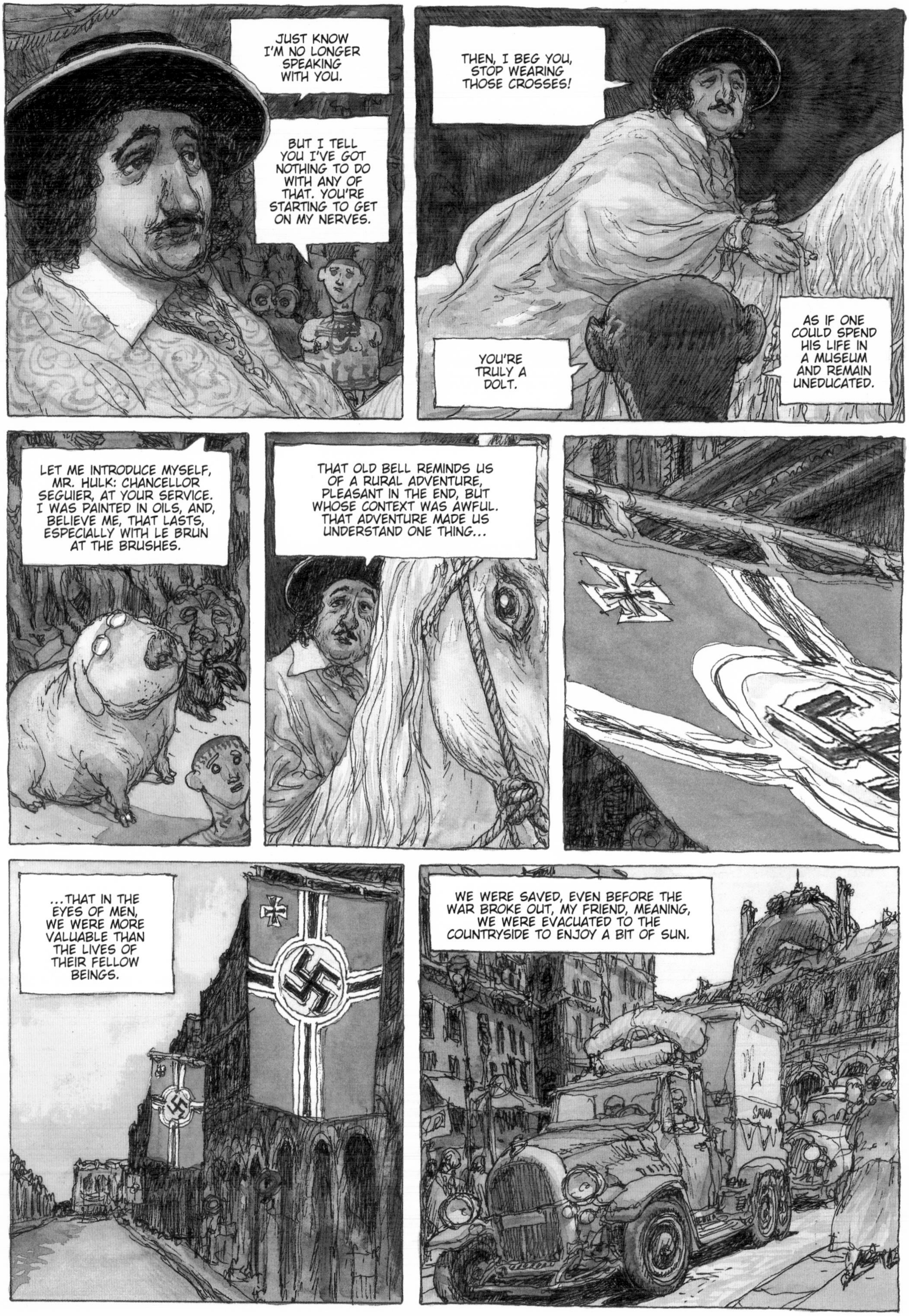
JUST KNOW I'M NO LONGER SPEAKING WITH YOU.
BUT I TELL YOU I'VE GOT NOTHING TO DO WITH ANY OF THAT. YOU'RE STARTING TO GET ON MY NERVES.
THEN, I BEG YOU, STOP WEARING THOSE CROSSES!
YOU'RE TRULY A DOLT.
AS IF ONE COULD SPEND HIS LIFE IN A MUSEUM AND REMAIN UNEDUCATED.
LET ME INTRODUCE MYSELF, MR. HULK: CHANCELLOR SEGUIER, AT YOUR SERVICE. I WAS PAINTED IN OILS, AND, BELIEVE ME, THAT LASTS, ESPECIALLY WITH LE BRUN AT THE BRUSHES.
THAT OLD BELL REMINDS US OF A RURAL ADVENTURE, PLEASANT IN THE END, BUT WHOSE CONTEXT WAS AWFUL. THAT ADVENTURE MADE US UNDERSTAND ONE THING...
...THAT IN THE EYES OF MEN, WE WERE MORE VALUABLE THAN THE LIVES OF THEIR FELLOW BEINGS.
WE WERE SAVED, EVEN BEFORE THE WAR BROKE OUT, MY FRIEND, MEANING, WE WERE EVACUATED TO THE COUNTRYSIDE TO ENJOY A BIT OF SUN.

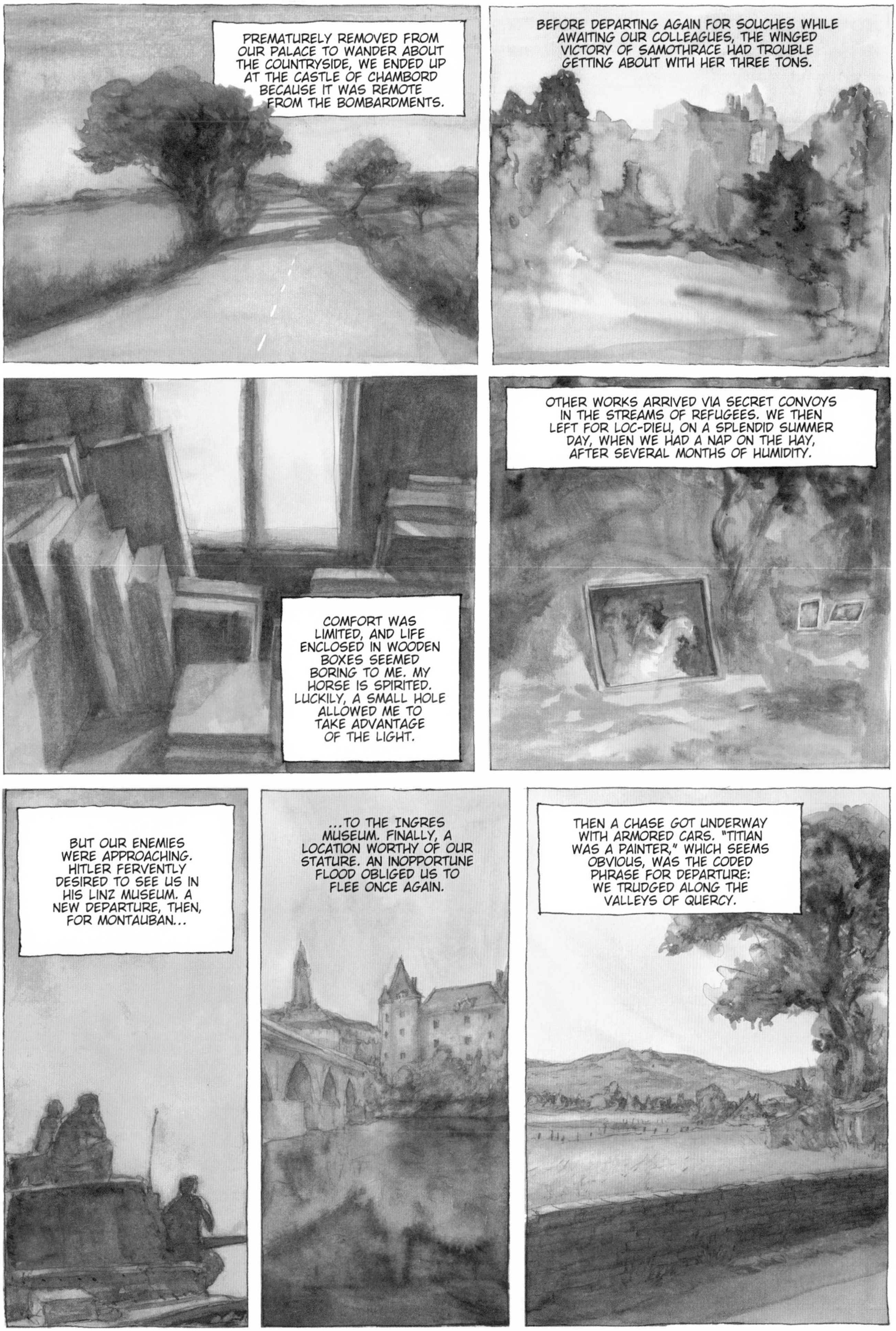
PREMATURELY REMOVED FROM OUR PALACE TO WANDER ABOUT THE COUNTRYSIDE, WE ENDED UP AT THE CASTLE OF CHAMBORD BECAUSE IT WAS REMOTE FROM THE BOMBARDMENTS.
BEFORE DEPARTING AGAIN FOR SOUCHES WHILE AWAITING OUR COLLEAGUES, THE WINGED VICTORY OF SAMOTHRACE HAD TROUBLE GETTING ABOUT WITH HER THREE TONS.
COMFORT WAS LIMITED, AND LIFE ENCLOSED IN WOODEN BOXES SEEMED BORING TO ME. MY HORSE IS SPIRITED. LUCKILY, A SMALL HOLE ALLOWED ME TO TAKE ADVANTAGE OF THE LIGHT.
OTHER WORKS ARRIVED VIA SECRET CONVOYS IN THE STREAMS OF REFUGEES. WE THEN LEFT FOR LOC-DIEU, ON A SPLENDID SUMMER DAY, WHEN WE HAD A NAP ON THE HAY, AFTER SEVERAL MONTHS OF HUMIDITY.
BUT OUR ENEMIES WERE APPROACHING. HITLER FERVENTLY DESIRED TO SEE US IN HIS LINZ MUSEUM. A NEW DEPARTURE, THEN, FOR MONTAUBAN...
...TO THE INGRES MUSEUM. FINALLY, A LOCATION WORTHY OF OUR STATURE. AN INOPPORTUNE FLOOD OBLIGED US TO FLEE ONCE AGAIN.
THEN A CHASE GOT UNDERWAY WITH ARMORED CARS. "TITIAN WAS A PAINTER," WHICH SEEMS OBVIOUS, WAS THE CODED PHRASE FOR DEPARTURE: WE TRUDGED ALONG THE VALLEYS OF QUERCY.

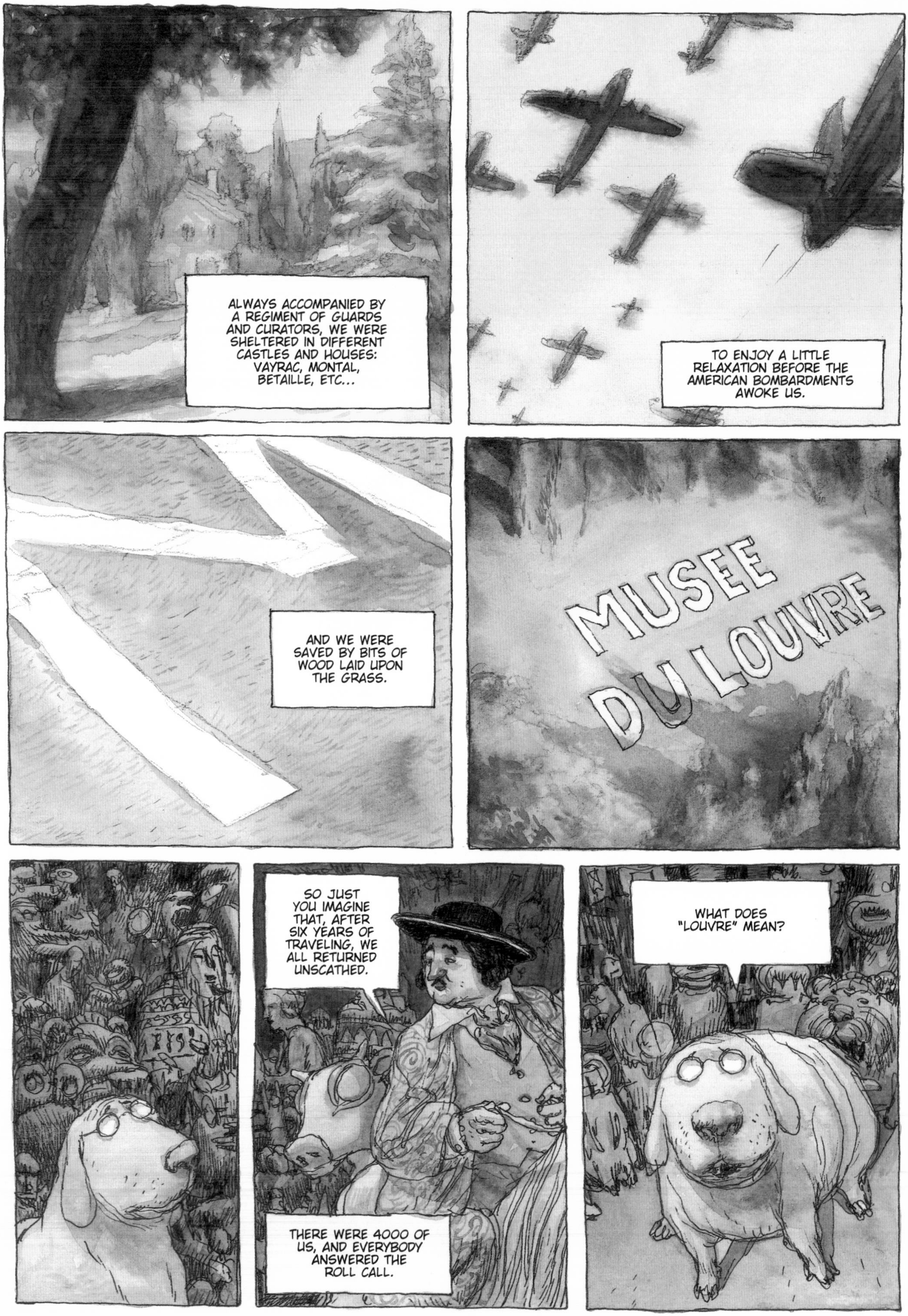
ALWAYS ACCOMPANIED BY A REGIMENT OF GUARDS AND CURATORS, WE WERE SHELTERED IN DIFFERENT CASTLES AND HOUSES: VAYRAC, MONTAL, BETAILLE, ETC...
TO ENJOY A LITTLE RELAXATION BEFORE THE AMERICAN BOMBARDMENTS AWOKE US.
AND WE WERE SAVED BY BITS OF WOOD LAID UPON THE GRASS.
MUSEE DU LOUVRE
SO JUST YOU IMAGINE THAT, AFTER SIX YEARS OF TRAVELING, WE ALL RETURNED UNSCATHED.
THERE WERE 4000 OF US, AND EVERYBODY ANSWERED THE ROLL CALL.
WHAT DOES "LOUVRE" MEAN?

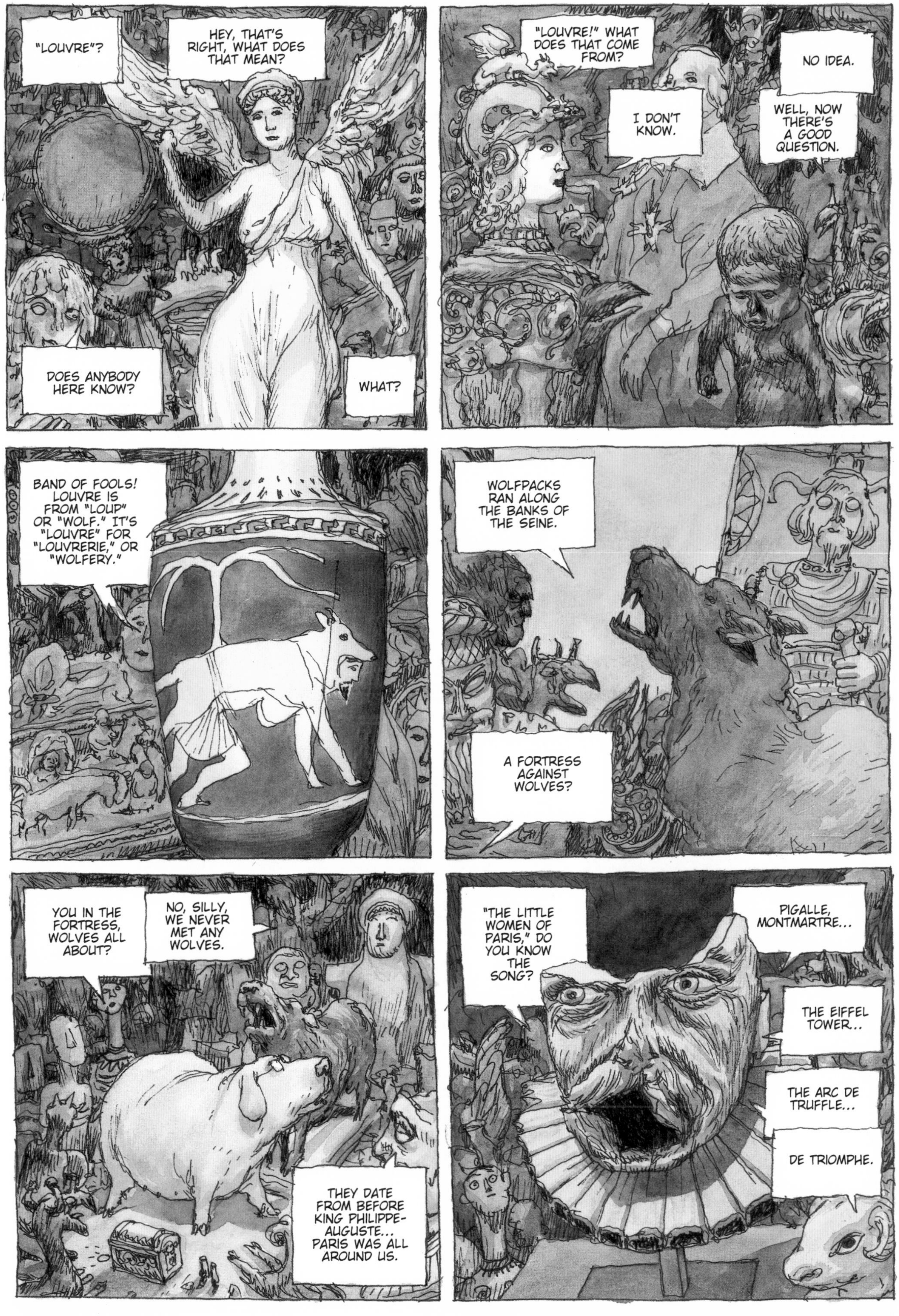
"LOUVRE"?
HEY, THAT'S RIGHT, WHAT DOES THAT MEAN?
DOES ANYBODY HERE KNOW?
WHAT?
"LOUVRE!" WHAT DOES THAT COME FROM?
I DON'T KNOW.
NO IDEA.
WELL, NOW THERE'S A GOOD QUESTION.
BAND OF FOOLS! LOUVRE IS FROM "LOUP" OR "WOLF." IT'S "LOUVRE" FOR "LOUVRERIE," OR "WOLFERY."
WOLFPACKS RAN ALONG THE BANKS OF THE SEINE.
A FORTRESS AGAINST WOLVES?
YOU IN THE FORTRESS, WOLVES ALL ABOUT?
NO, SILLY, WE NEVER MET ANY WOLVES.
THEY DATE FROM BEFORE KING PHILIPPE-AUGUSTE... PARIS WAS ALL AROUND US.
"THE LITTLE WOMEN OF PARIS," DO YOU KNOW THE SONG?
PIGALLE, MONTMARTRE...
THE EIFFEL TOWER...
THE ARC DE TRUFFLE...
DE TRIOMPHE.

PEOPLE IN THE HUNDREDS OF THOUSANDS WOULD COME TO SEE US. IT WAS COOL.

'SEE US'? MAYBE...

LET'S JUST SAY THEY WOULD LOOK AT US WHILE WAITING IN LINE TO ADMIRE THE "THREE RED DOTS."

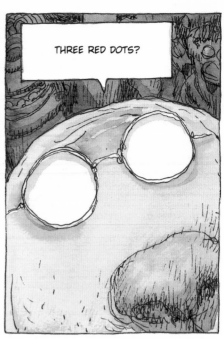

THREE RED DOTS?

WE'VE BEEN CALLING HER THAT SINCE OUR TRIP TO THE COUNTRY-SIDE.

THERE WERE THREE RED DOTS ON HER BOX: "NATIONAL TREASURE"!

THE SUPER STAR HERE.

YOU ALWAYS HAVE TO HAVE A STAR TO GET THE OBESE TO COME OUT.

THREE RED DOTS. SEE HOW SHE RUNS.

I CALL HER CASIMIR.

CASIMIR MALEVITCH.

SHE FADED AWAY, WITHDRAWN FROM SIGHT, NO DOUBT WORN OUT BY TOO MUCH EXHIBITION. TODAY, SHE'S JUST A WHITE SQUARE ON A WHITE BACKGROUND.

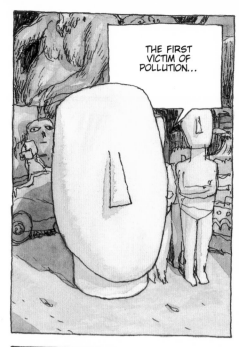

THE FIRST VICTIM OF POLLUTION...

...A RAPID POLLUTION. IN FIFTY YEARS, WE OBSERVED A CHANGE IN THE MORPHOLOGY OF HUMANS, MAXIMUM YIELD FROM ENERGY, A GENERAL INCREASE IN WASTE AND FAT.

AT THE BEGINNING OF THE TWENTIETH CENTURY, WE'D STILL SEE THE INSPIRED, SKINNY ONES.

AT THE BEGINNING OF THE TWENTY-FIRST, IT WAS ALREADY THE ERA OF THE FAT, JOLLY ONES.

THERE WAS GLOBAL WARMING. THE PHENOMENON THEY'D PREDICTED CAME ABOUT MORE QUICKLY THAN EXPECTED.

THOSE WHO RESISTED -THERE WEREN'T MANY- FLED TOWARDS THE SOUTH.

WE REMAINED HERE ALONE.

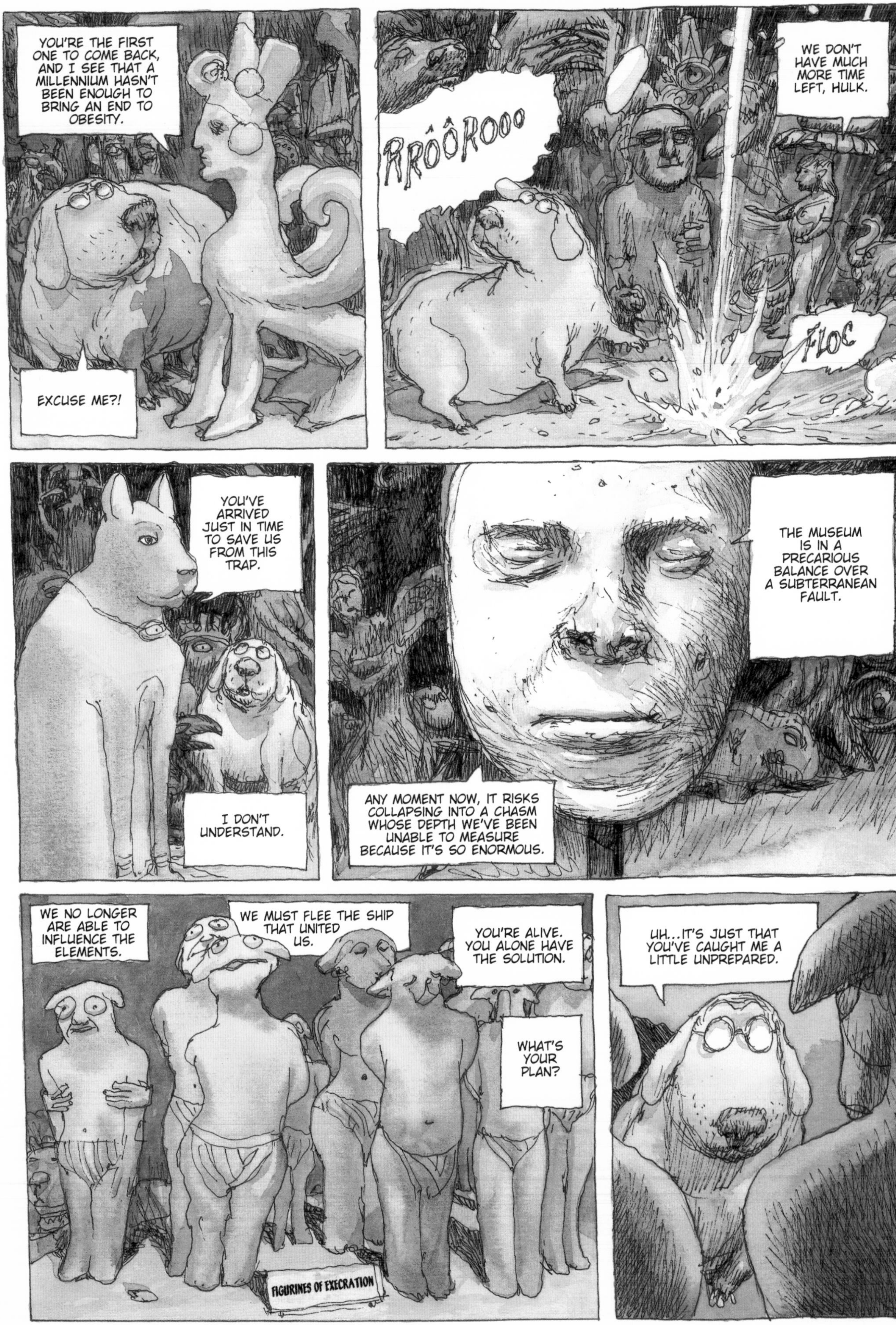
YOU'RE THE FIRST ONE TO COME BACK, AND I SEE THAT A MILLENNIUM HASN'T BEEN ENOUGH TO BRING AN END TO OBESITY.
EXCUSE ME?!
RRÔÔROOO
WE DON'T HAVE MUCH MORE TIME LEFT, HULK.
FLOC
YOU'VE ARRIVED JUST IN TIME TO SAVE US FROM THIS TRAP.
I DON'T UNDERSTAND.
THE MUSEUM IS IN A PRECARIOUS BALANCE OVER A SUBTERRANEAN FAULT.
ANY MOMENT NOW, IT RISKS COLLAPSING INTO A CHASM WHOSE DEPTH WE'VE BEEN UNABLE TO MEASURE BECAUSE IT'S SO ENORMOUS.
WE NO LONGER ARE ABLE TO INFLUENCE THE ELEMENTS.
WE MUST FLEE THE SHIP THAT UNITED US.
YOU'RE ALIVE. YOU ALONE HAVE THE SOLUTION.
WHAT'S YOUR PLAN?
FIGURINES OF EXECRATION
UH...IT'S JUST THAT YOU'VE CAUGHT ME A LITTLE UNPREPARED.

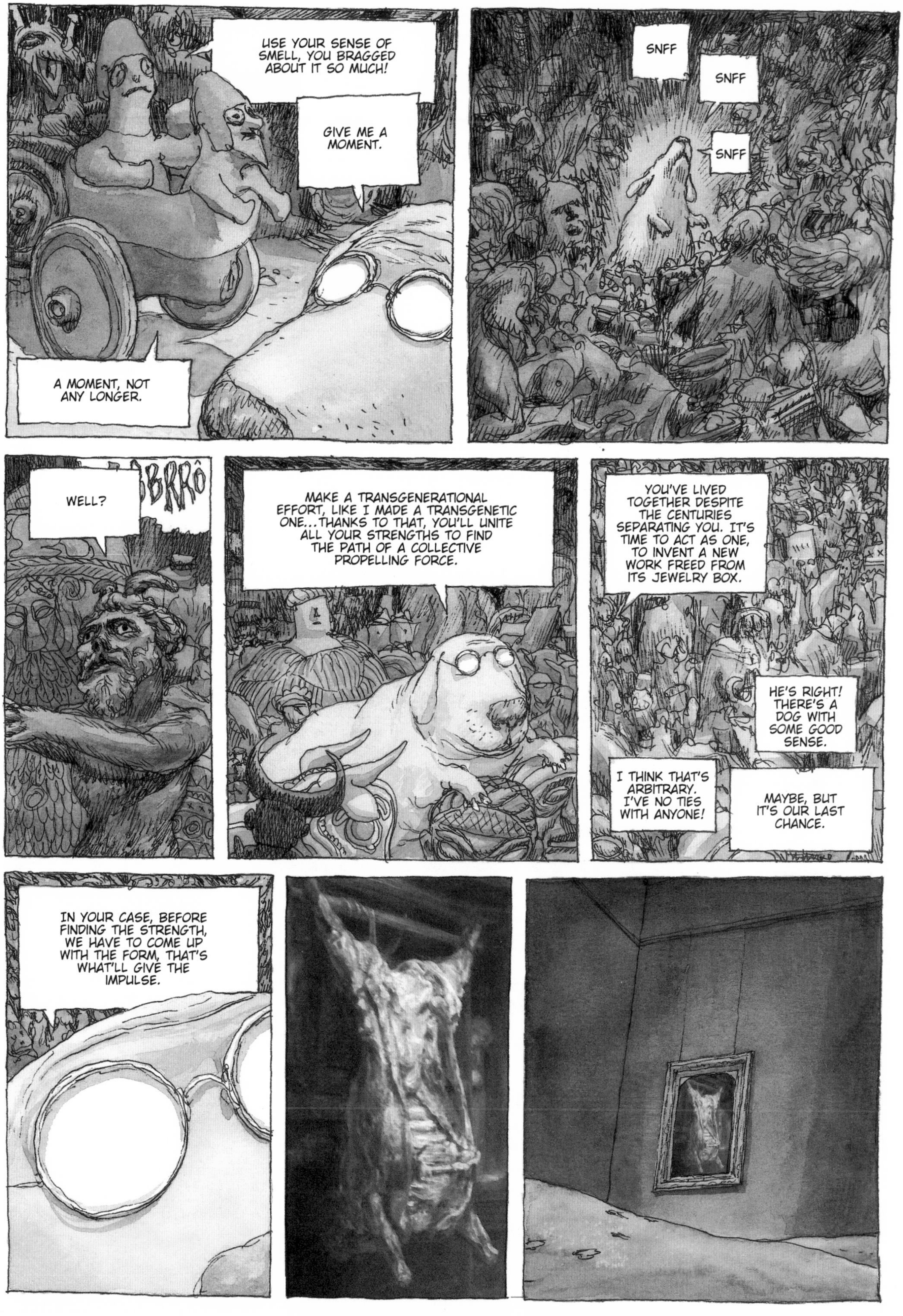
USE YOUR SENSE OF SMELL, YOU BRAGGED ABOUT IT SO MUCH!
GIVE ME A MOMENT.
A MOMENT, NOT ANY LONGER.
SNFF
SNFF
SNFF
WELL?
MAKE A TRANSGENERATIONAL EFFORT, LIKE I MADE A TRANSGENETIC ONE...THANKS TO THAT, YOU'LL UNITE ALL YOUR STRENGTHS TO FIND THE PATH OF A COLLECTIVE PROPELLING FORCE.
YOU'VE LIVED TOGETHER DESPITE THE CENTURIES SEPARATING YOU. IT'S TIME TO ACT AS ONE, TO INVENT A NEW WORK FREED FROM ITS JEWELRY BOX.
HE'S RIGHT! THERE'S A DOG WITH SOME GOOD SENSE.
I THINK THAT'S ARBITRARY. I'VE NO TIES WITH ANYONE!
MAYBE, BUT IT'S OUR LAST CHANCE.
IN YOUR CASE, BEFORE FINDING THE STRENGTH, WE HAVE TO COME UP WITH THE FORM, THAT'S WHAT'LL GIVE THE IMPULSE.

I'M COLD.

?!

!!

DON'T BE AFRAID.

I AM BES. I'LL PROTECT YOU, THAT'S MY JOB. I WATCH OVER THE WEAK AND DANCING WOMEN, AND I KEEP EVIL SPIRITS OUT OF YOUR DREAMS.

HULK PUT ME IN CHARGE OF COMING TO LOOK FOR YOU. GIVE ME YOUR HAND.

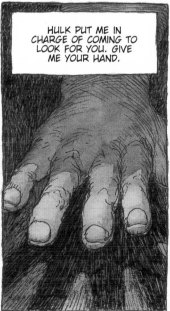

72

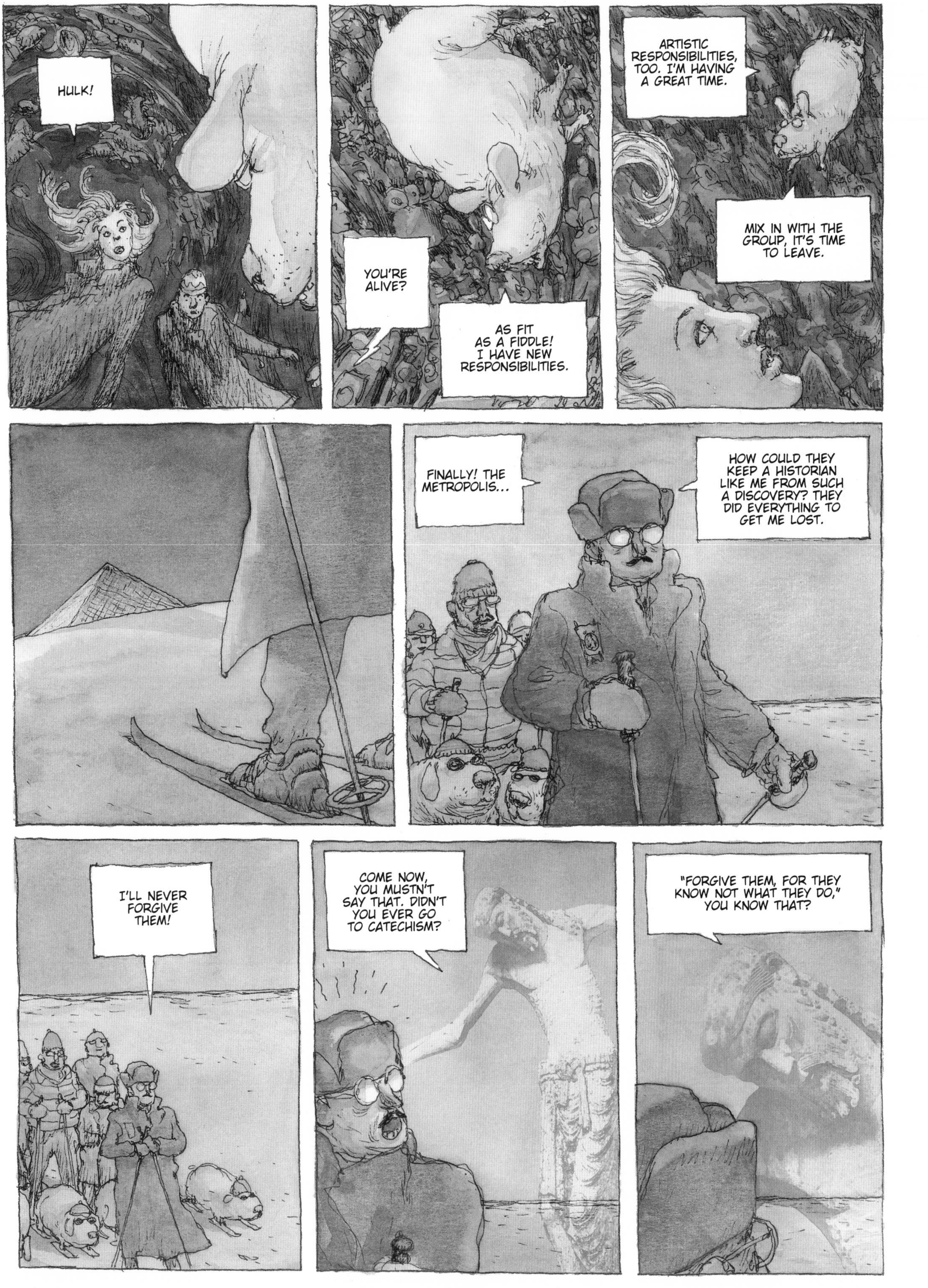
HULK!
YOU'RE ALIVE?
AS FIT AS A FIDDLE! I HAVE NEW RESPONSIBILITIES.
ARTISTIC RESPONSIBILITIES, TOO. I'M HAVING A GREAT TIME.
MIX IN WITH THE GROUP, IT'S TIME TO LEAVE.
FINALLY! THE METROPOLIS...
HOW COULD THEY KEEP A HISTORIAN LIKE ME FROM SUCH A DISCOVERY? THEY DID EVERYTHING TO GET ME LOST.
I'LL NEVER FORGIVE THEM!
COME NOW, YOU MUSTN'T SAY THAT. DIDN'T YOU EVER GO TO CATECHISM?
"FORGIVE THEM, FOR THEY KNOW NOT WHAT THEY DO," YOU KNOW THAT?

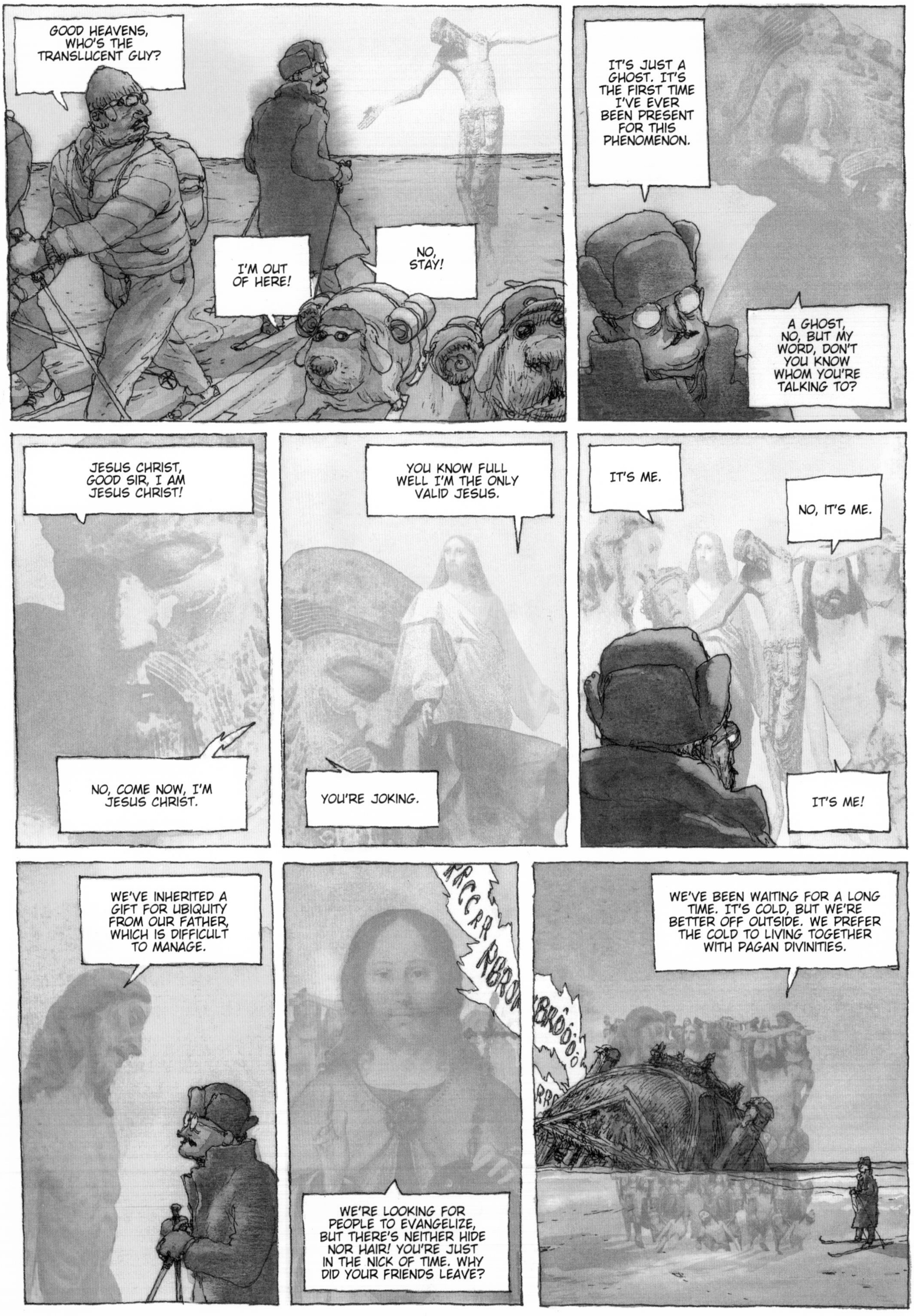
GOOD HEAVENS, WHO'S THE TRANSLUCENT GUY?
I'M OUT OF HERE!
NO, STAY!
IT'S JUST A GHOST. IT'S THE FIRST TIME I'VE EVER BEEN PRESENT FOR THIS PHENOMENON.
A GHOST, NO, BUT MY WORD, DON'T YOU KNOW WHOM YOU'RE TALKING TO?
JESUS CHRIST, GOOD SIR, I AM JESUS CHRIST!
NO, COME NOW, I'M JESUS CHRIST.
YOU KNOW FULL WELL I'M THE ONLY VALID JESUS.
YOU'RE JOKING.
IT'S ME.
NO, IT'S ME.
IT'S ME!
WE'VE INHERITED A GIFT FOR UBIQUITY FROM OUR FATHER, WHICH IS DIFFICULT TO MANAGE.
WE'RE LOOKING FOR PEOPLE TO EVANGELIZE, BUT THERE'S NEITHER HIDE NOR HAIR! YOU'RE JUST IN THE NICK OF TIME. WHY DID YOUR FRIENDS LEAVE?
WE'VE BEEN WAITING FOR A LONG TIME. IT'S COLD, BUT WE'RE BETTER OFF OUTSIDE. WE PREFER THE COLD TO LIVING TOGETHER WITH PAGAN DIVINITIES.

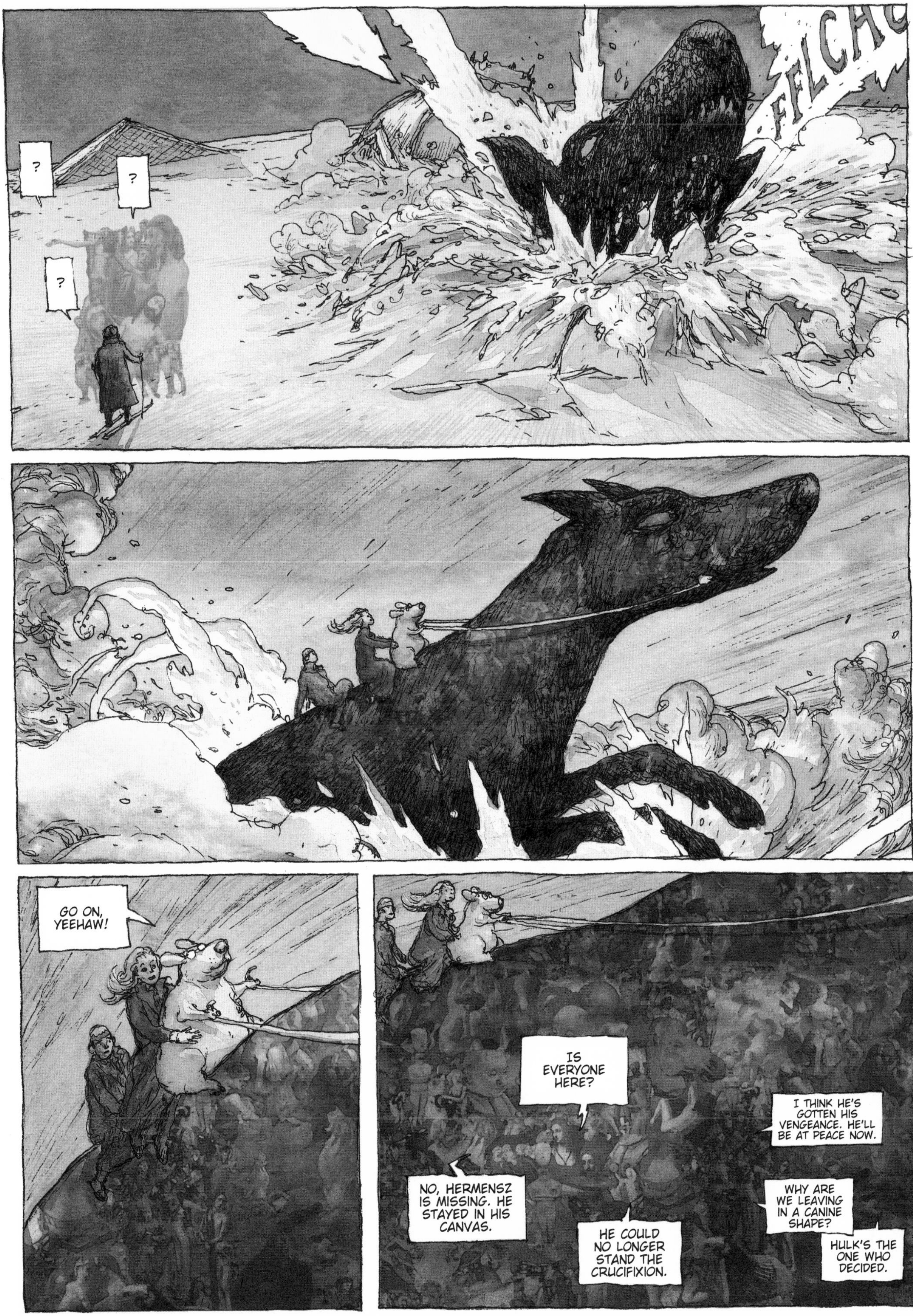
?
?
?
FFLCHC
GO ON, YEEHAW!
IS EVERYONE HERE?
I THINK HE'S GOTTEN HIS VENGEANCE. HE'LL BE AT PEACE NOW.
NO, HERMENSZ IS MISSING. HE STAYED IN HIS CANVAS.
HE COULD NO LONGER STAND THE CRUCIFIXION.
WHY ARE WE LEAVING IN A CANINE SHAPE?
HULK'S THE ONE WHO DECIDED.

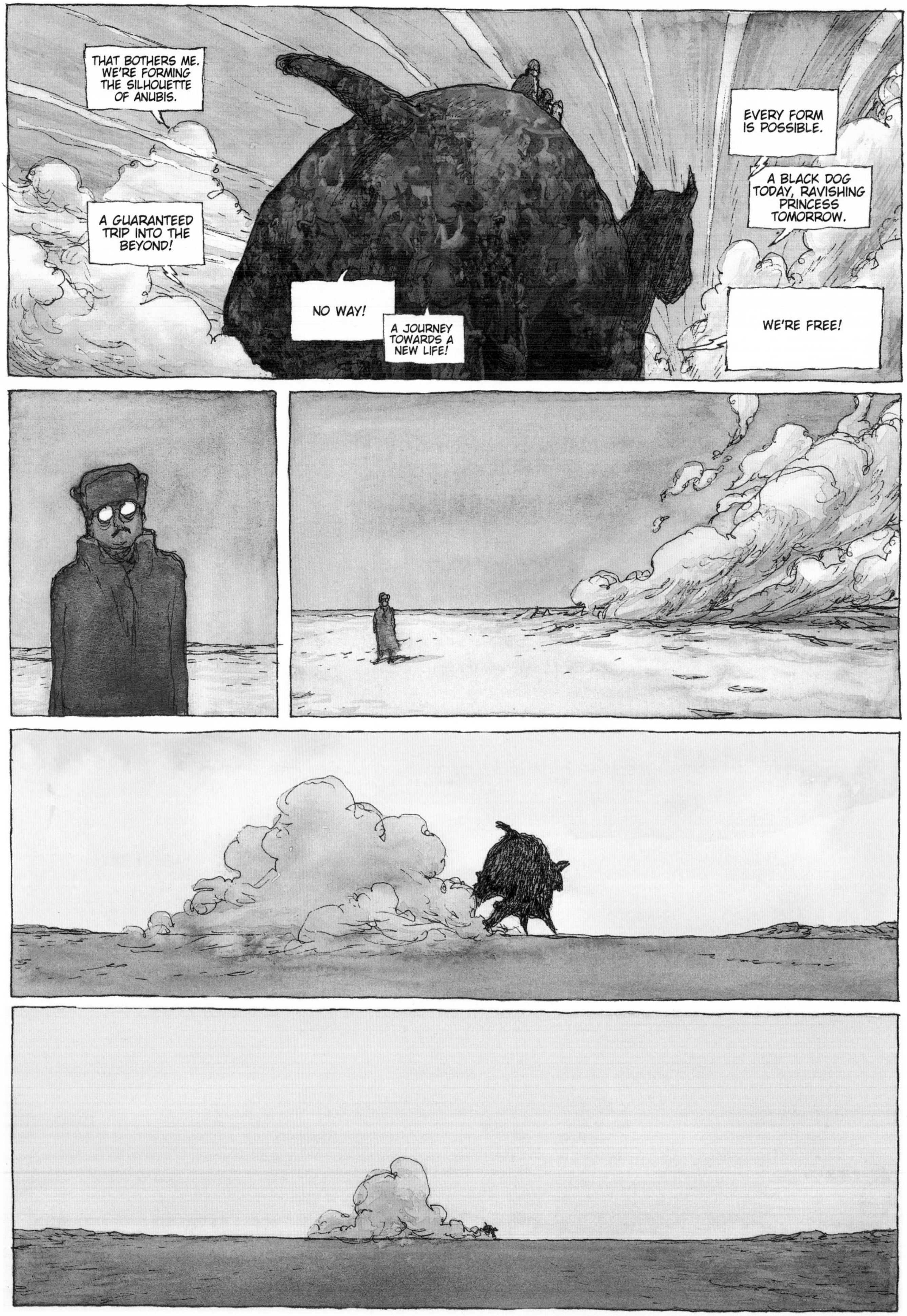
THAT BOTHERS ME. WE'RE FORMING THE SILHOUETTE OF ANUBIS.
A GUARANTEED TRIP INTO THE BEYOND!
NO WAY!
A JOURNEY TOWARDS A NEW LIFE!
EVERY FORM IS POSSIBLE.
A BLACK DOG TODAY, RAVISHING PRINCESS TOMORROW.
WE'RE FREE!

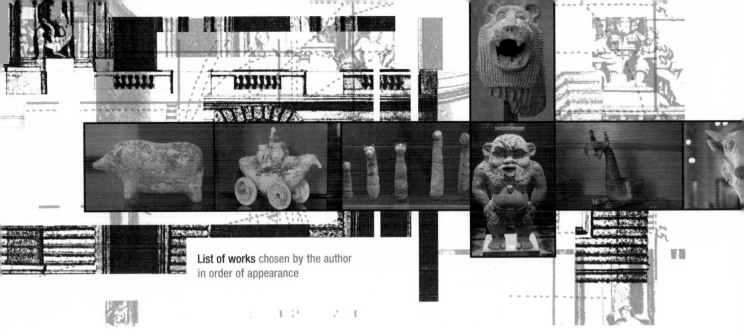

List of works chosen by the author in order of appearance

Page 27
Protome of a griffon
First third of the 6th century
Decorated Fire-dog?, Br 3685
Denon Pavilion, Ground floor, Room 18

Page 34
Louis Hersent
The Monks of Saint Gothard
Salon de 1824
Oil on canvas, 134 cm x 138 cm., Inv. 5328
Sully Pavilion, Third floor, Room 66.

Page 35
Jean-Frédéric Schall
The Comparison
Oil on canvas, 40 cm x 32 cm
Hélène and Victor Lyon Donation 1961, RF 1961-75
Sully Pavilion, Third floor, Room C

Page 36
Eugène Delacroix
A Smoking Turk, seated on a divan, 1825?
Oil on canvas, 25 cm x 30 cm
Étienne Moreau-Nélaton Donation 1906, RF 1656
Sully Pavilion, Third Floor, Room 71

Page 38
Eugène Delacroix
Study of a nude woman, lying on a divan, known as The Woman with white stockings, circa 1825-1830
Oil on canvas, 26 cm x 33 cm
Étienne Moreau Nélaton Donation 1906
Sully Pavilion, Third Floor, room 71

Eugène Delacroix
Hamlet and Ophelia, 1840
Oil on canvas, 29 cm x 22 cm
Étienne Moreau Nélaton bequest, 1927, RF 2638
Sully Pavilion, Third Floor, Room 71

Page 39
Alexandre-Gabriel Decamps
The Monkey painter, also known as *Studio interior,* circa 1833
Oil on canvas, 32 cm x 40 cm
Thomy Thiéry bequest, 1902, RF 1375
Sully Pavilion, Third Floor, Room 72

Page 42
Antonio Canal, known as **Canaletto**
The Church of the Salute
Oil on canvas, 119 cm x 153 cm, RF 1961-33
Sully Pavilion, Third Floor, Room C

Eugène Delacroix
Saint George battling the dragon or *Perseus rescuing Andromeda,* 1847
Canvas, 28 cm x 36 cm
Thomy Thiéry bequest, 1902, RF 1396
Sully Pavilion, Third Floor, Room 72

Page 43
John Constable
Weymouth Bay at the approach of a storm, circa 1819-1827
Oil on canvas, 88 cm x 112 cm, RF 39
Sully Pavilion, Second Floor, Room 74

Page 44
Jean-Baptiste Camille Corot
Vesuvius, 1828
Oil on canvas, 24 cm x 41 cm
Étienne Moreau Nélaton Donation, 1906
Sully Pavilion, Third Floor, Room 69

Jean-Baptiste Camille Corot
Fishermen Houses in Saint Adresse (Seine-Maritime), circa 1830-1840
Oil on canvas, 28 cm x 42 cm
Étienne Moreau Nélaton Donation, 1906
Sully Pavilion, Third Floor, Room 69

Hieronymus Bosch
The Ship of Fools, after 1491
Oil on wood, 58 cm x 32 cm
Camille Benoit Donation, 1918, RF 2218
Richelieu Pavilion, Third Floor, Room 5

Francesco Guardi
View of La Giudecca with the Zattere, circa 1780
Oil on canvas, 34 cm x 53 cm
Othon Kaufmann et François Schlageter Gift, 1983, RF 1983-62
Denon Pavilion, Second Floor, Room 23

Claude Gellée, known as **Le Lorrain**
Seaport at sunset, 1639
Oil on canvas, 103 cm x 137 cm
Louis XIV Collection (gift of Le Nôtre in 1693), Inv 4715
Richelieu Pavilion, Third Floor, Room 15

Eugène Delacroix
The Death of Sardanapalus, 1827
Oil on canvas, 342 cm x 496 cm
Acquired in 1921, RF 2346
Denon Pavilion, Second Floor, Room 77

Pierre Paul Prud'hon
Venus, marriage and love, circa 1793
Oil on canvas, 44 cm x 33 cm
On loan from the Musée des Beaux-Arts d'Alger, 1970, DL 1970-18
Sully Pavilion, Third Floor, Room 56

François André Vincent
Zeuxis and the girls of Crotone, 1789
Oil on canvas, 325 cm x 415 cm
Louis XVI Collection, Inv 8453
Sully Pavilion, Third Floor, Room 53

Page 45
François Boucher
The Odalisk, 1745
Oil on canvas, 53.5 cm x 64.5 cm
Bequest of Baron Basile de Schlinchting, 1914, RF 2140
Sully Pavilion, Third Floor, Room 40

Jean-Auguste Dominique Ingres
Angelique (detail), circa 1819
Canvas, 85 cm x 143 cm
Bequest of Paul Cosson, 1926, RF 2520
Sully Pavilion, Third Floor, Room 60

Jean-Siméon Chardin
The Monkey Painter, 1739-1740
Oil on canvas, 73 cm x 59 cm
Bequest of Dr. Louis La Caze, 1869, MI 1033
Sully Pavilion, Third Floor, Room 39

Domenico Mecarino, known as **Beccafumi**
Saint Anthony and the miracle of the mule
Oil on canvas, 33 cm x 51 cm
Acquired in 1966, RF 1966-2
Denon Pavilion, Second Floor, Room 8

Jacob Jordaens
Diana resting, circa 1640-1650
Oil on canvas, 203 cm x 264 cm
Gift of the Society of Friends of the Museum, 1982, RF 1982-11
Richelieu Pavilion, Third Floor, Room 26

Antonio Allegri, known as **Corregio**
Venus and Eros discovered by a satyr, once known as *Jupiter and Antiope,* circa 1524-1525
Oil on canvas, 188 cm x 125 cm
Acquired by Louis XIV from the heirs of Mazarin, 1665, Inv 42
Denon Pavilion, Second Floor, Room 8

Petrus-Paulus Rubens
The Virgin and Child, surrounded by the Innocents, once titled *Virgin with Children*
Oil on canvas, 138 cm x 100 cm
Collection of Louis XIV, acquired in 1671, Inv 1763
Richelieu Pavilion, Third Floor, Room 21

Nicolas Poussin
The Spring, (reversed detail), circa 1660-1664
Oil on canvas, 118 cm x 160 cm
Collection of Louis XIV, acquired by the Duke of Richelieu in 1665, Inv 7303
Richelieu Pavilion, Third Floor, Room 16

Stefano di Giovanni di Console, known as **Sassetta**
The Fortunate Ranieri Rasini delivers the poor from a prison in Florence, between 1437 and 1444
Oil on canvas, 43 cm x 63 cm
Gift of the Society for Friends of the Louvre, 1965, RF 1965-2
Denon Pavilion, Second Floor, Room 4

Sano di Pietro
The death of the saint and his appearance to Saint Cyril of Jerusalem
Belongs to *Scenes of the life of Saint Jerome,* 1444
Oil on wood, 23 cm x 35 cm, MI 473
Denon Pavilion, Second Floor, Room of the Sept-Mètres

Page 46
Carlo Braccesco
The Annunciation, central panel of a triptych, circa 1480-1500
Oil on wood, 158 cm x 107 cm
Acquired in 1812, Inv 1410
Denon Pavilion, Second Floor, Room 5

François Boucher
The Kidnapping of Europa (detail), 1747
Canvas, 160 cm x 193 cm
Collection of Louis XV, acquired in 1747, Inv 2714
Sully Pavilion, Third Floor, Room 46

Francesco di Stefano, known as **Pesellino**
The Stigmatization of Saint Francis, circa 1440-1445
Oil on wood, 32 cm x 94 cm.
Received in the Louvre in 1814, Inv 418
Denon Pavilion, Second Floor, Room 4

Pietro di Cristoforo Vannucci, known as **Perugino**
Saint Jerome saves two hanged men
(right panel of a triptych), circa 1473-1475
Oil on wood, 30 cm x 28 cm
Ancient Campana Collection, Rome, Louvre 1863, MI 481
Denon Pavilion, Second Floor, Room 4

Nicolaes Maes
The Bathing
Oil on cavas, 72 cm x 91 cm
Bequest of Baron Basile de Schlichting, 1914, RF 2132
Richelieu Pavilion, Third Floor, Room 32

Ferdinand Bol
The Noble children (of the Trip family?) in goat-drawn cart, 1654
Oil on canvas, 211 cm x 249 cm.
Séquestre Miliotty, 1799, Inv 1062
Richelieu Pavilion, Third Floor, Room 33

Liberale da Verona
The Kidnapping of Europa, circa 1470
Painted panel, 39 cm x 118 cm
Former Campana collection, received in the Louvre in 1863, MI 585
Denon Pavilion, Second Floor, Room 4

Joos van Craesbeek
The Smoker
Oil on canvas, 41 cm x 32 cm
Bequest of Dr. Louis La Caze, 1869, MI 906
Richelieu Pavilion, Third Floor, Room 23

Michael Wutky
Eruption of Vesuvius, circa 1780
Oil on cavas, 78 cm x 64 cm
Acquired in 1998 due to the sponsorship of the Saint Gobain Company, RF 1998-37
Richelieu Pavilion, Third Floor, Room F

Maître des anges rebelles (Master of the Rebellious Angels)
The Fall of the rebellious angels,

circa 1340-1345
Distemper on wood set on canvas, 64 cm x 29 cm
On loan from the Bourges Museum, 1967, D.L. 1967-1-b
Denon Pavilion, Second Floor, Room 4

PAGE 47
Antonio Carracci
The Deluge, circa 1616-1618
Canvas, 166 cm x 247 cm
Collection of Louis XIV (gift of the heirs of Cardinal Mazarin in 1661), Inv 230
Denon Pavilion, Second Floor, Room 12

Eugène Delacroix
Dante and Virgil in the Inferno, also known as
Dante's Boat (detail), salon of 1822
Oil on canvas, 189 cm x 241 cm
Acquired at the Salon of 1822, Inv 3820
Denon Pavilion, Second Floor, Room 77

Théodore Géricault
The Tempest, or *the Flotsam*
Oil on canvas, 19 cm x 25 cm, RF 784
Sully Pavilion, Third Floor, Room 61

Joachim Wtewael
Perseus rescuing Andromeda (detail), 1611
Oil on canvas, 180 cm x 150 cm
Gift of the Society of Friends of the Musée du Louvre, 1982, P, RF 1982-51
Richelieu Pavilion, Third Floor, Room 13

Raffaelo Santi, known as **Raphael**
Saint Michael (detail), circa 1504
Oil on wood, 30.9 cm x 26.5 cm
Collection of Louis XIV (acquired in 1661), Inv 608
Denon Pavilion, Second Floor, Room 5

Caspar David Friedrich
Seacoast by moonlight, 1818
Oil on canvas, 22 x 30 cm
Gift of the Society of Friends of the Louvre, RF 2000-3
Richelieu Pavilion, Third Floor, Room E

Claude Monet
Ice on the Seine at Bougival
Oil on canvas, 65 cm x 81 cm
Hélène and Victor Lyon Donation, 1961, RF 1961-62
Sully Pavilion, Third Floor, Room C

Jean-Siméon Chardin
The Stingray, before 1728
Oil on canvas, 114 cm x 146 cm
Collection of the Académie, Inv. 3197
Sully Pavilion, Second Floor, Room 38

PAGE 50
Hermes putting on a sandal,
Roman work, 2nd century A.D.
Discovered in the Theatre of Marcellus in Rome. Marble of Pentelichus for the body, 161 cm. Received in the Louvre in 1797, MR 238/Ma 83
Sully Pavilion, Ground floor, Room 17.

Edmé Bouchardon
Sleeping faun, 1726-30
Marble, 184 cm x 142 cm x 119 cm
Received in the Louvre in 1892
Richelieu Pavilion, Mezzanine, Puget Court

PAGE 51
The Three Graces, Roman work of the Imperial era, 2nd century, A.D.(?)
Rome, Mount Cellius, Villa Cornovaglia
Marble, 119 cm x 85 cm
Former Borghese Collection in Rome, purchased in 1807, MR 211/Ma 287
Sully Pavilion, Ground floor, Room 17

Old man skinning an animal, known as *"The Rustic Skinner,"*
Roman work of the Imperial era, 1st or 2nd century A.D.
Marble, 107 cm
Former Albani Collection, seized by Napoleon, re-purchased by Louis XVIII in 1815, Ma 517
Sully Pavilion, Ground floor, Room 17

Child and goose, Roman work of the Imperial era, 1st or 2nd century, A.D., Discovered in 1792 in the Villa Quintili in Rome
Marble, 92.7 cm
Former Braschi Collection in Rome, seized by Napoleon by virtue of the Treaty of Tolentino in 1797, Received in the Louvre in 1799, Ma 40
Sully Pavilion, Ground floor, Room 17

PAGE 52
Rhyton with a bull's head, Late Minoan, 1400-1200, B.C.
Terracotta, 16.4 cm x 16 cm
Clermont-Ganneau Mission, 1896, CA 909
Denon Pavilion, Mezzanine, Room 1

PAGE 53
Pig, from Cyrenaica
5.1 cm x 9.6 cm
Vattier de Bourville Acquisition, 1851
Sully Pavilion, Second Floor, Room 36

PAGE 55
Animal shown loaded with amphorae, 700-650 B.C.
19 cm x 25 cm
Acquisition 1910, CA 1841
Sully Pavilion, Second Floor, Room 36

PAGE 56
Head of Lion-Temple guard, beginning of the second millennium B.C., Babylon
Terracotta
Acquired in 1947, AO 19807
Richelieu Pavilion, Ground floor, Room 3

Cat mummies
52.5 cm x 13 cm, N 2889, E 2811, N 2812, N 3505
Sully Pavilion, Ground floor, Room 19

Androcephalous winged bulls, 721-705 B.C.
Khorsabad, Palace of Sargon II of Assyria
Gypsum, 420 cm x 436 cm
P. E. Botta Excavation, 1843-44, AO 19857
Richelieu Pavilion, Ground floor, Room 4

PAGE 57
Canopic jar, Second half of the 6th century, B.C., Chiusi, Italy.
Terracotta, 50 cm
Purchased 1851, D 162
Denon Pavilion, Ground floor, Room 19

Lid of masculine canopic jar
First half of the 6th century, B.C., D 163
Denon Pavilion, Ground floor, Room 19

Assyrian hero mastering a lion
Khorsabad, Palace of Sargon II of Assyria
450 cm x 188 cm x 22 cm
P. E. Botta Excavation 1843-44, AO 19861
Richelieu Pavilion, Ground floor, Room 4

Four canopic jars of Horemsaf
Late Period, 664-332 B.C.
Egyptian alabaster, 36.5 cm
E 18876, E 18877, E 18879
Sully Pavilion, Ground floor, Room 15

PAGE 58
Oenochoe in the form of a woman's head, circa 310-290 B.C.
61.5 cm x 21.7 cm
Campana Collection, 1861, B 489
Sully Pavilion, Second Floor, Room 37

Aphrodite standing on a goose, circa 500-475 B.C.
Boetia, 222 cm x 18.5 cm
Picard Gift, 1908, CA 1747
Sully Pavilion, Second Floor, Room 36

Warrior from the vicinity of Viterbo, beginning of the 5th century B.C.
BR 4225
Denon Pavilion, Ground floor, Room 18

PAGE 60
Vincenzo Catena
Giangiorgio Trissino, circa 1525-27
Oil on canvas, 72 cm x 63 cm, RF 2098
Denon Pavilion, Second Floor, Grand Gallery, Room 5

Juste de Gand and **Pedro Berruguete**
Saint Jerome-Studiolo d'Urbino, circa 1476
Oil on wood, 116 cm x 68 cm
MI 649
Richelieu Pavilion, Third Floor, Room 6

PAGE 61
Rembrandt Harmensz van Rijn
The Skinned Ox, 1655
Oil on canvas, 94 cm x 69 cm
Acquired from the art collector and critic Louis Viardot, 1857, MI 169
Richelieu Pavilion, Third Floor, Room 31

PAGE 62
Marie-Guillemine Benoist
Portrait of a black woman, Salon of 1800
Oil on canvas, 81 cm x 65 cm, Inv. 2508
Sully Pavilion, Third Floor, Room 54

PAGE 63
Small bell-idol, Thebes
circa 700 B.C.
Terracotta, 33 cm
Sully Pavilion, Second Floor, Room 36

Idol with Chalcolithic eyes,
northern Syria, circa 3500 B.C.
AO 30002
Sully Pavilion, Ground floor, Room C

Charles Le Brun
Pierre Séguier, Chancellor of France
(1588-1672), circa 1655-61
Oil on canvas, 295 cm x 357 cm
Sully Pavilion, Third Floor, Room 31

PAGE 67
Winged Victory phainomeride ("with naked thighs")
150-100 B.C., Myrina, Tomb B, Myr 161 bis
Sully Pavilion, Second Floor, Room 38

Sardonyx ewer,
1st century, BC-1st century, A.D., additions from the 17th century
Setting: enameled gold, rubies; Pierre Delabarre, Paris, circa 1630
27.5 cm x 16.5 cm x 10.5 cm, MR 445
Denon Pavilion, Second Floor, Apollo Gallery, Room 66

Seated Divinities,
Attica, Greece, around the middle of the 7th century B.C.
Excavations by the Armée d'Orient, 1916
CA 2078 Eleonte (phitos 13)
Rayet Acquisition, 1874, MNB 543
Tanagra Acquisition, 1899, CA 1145
Thebes
Sully Pavilion, Second Floor, Room 36

Anonymous
Head found during the excavation of the Cour Carrée
beginning of the 17th century
Sully Pavilion, Saint-Louis Crypt

PAGE 68
The Torture of Marsyas,
Roman work of the Imperial era, 1st or 2nd century A.D.,
Discovered in Rome
Marble, 256 cm
Former Borghese collection in Rome, purchased 1807, MR 267/Ma 542
Sully Pavilion, Ground floor, Room 17

Aphrodite of the Capitoline type,
Roman work of the Imperial era, 1st century A.D.
Marble, 180 cm
Former Borghese collection, purchased in 1807, MR 369/Ma 335
Sully Pavilion, Ground floor, Room 17

Anthropomorphic oenochoe with engraved decorations, geometric and animal motifs,
710-670 B.C., Southern Etruria, or Territory of the Faleri
39.6 cm x 23 cm
Campana Collection ?, S 5047
Denon Pavilion, Ground floor, Room 18

Leonardo da Vinci
Mona Lisa, also known as *La Gioconda,* 1503-1510
Oil on poplar, 77 cm x 53 cm
Denon Pavilion, Second Floor, Room 7

Man's Head
Archaic dynasty II, circa 2700-2600 B.C.
Limestone, incrusted with shale and shell, 3.3 cm x 6.3 cm x 6.6 cm
Kahn Gift, 1949, AO 20113
Richelieu Pavilion, Ground floor, Room 1C

Pan
Roman work of the Imperial era, 2nd century A.D.
Marble of Mount Pentelicus, Athenian region ?, 158 cm
Borghese Collection purchased in 1807 by Napoleon, MR 313
Sully Pavilion, Ground floor, Room 17

PAGE 69
Head of a female figurine
Early Cycladic II (2700-2300 B.C.)
Keros, type of Spedos marble, 27 cm
Rayet Gift, 1873, Ma 2709
Denon Pavilion, Mezzanine, Room 1

Aphrodite ?
circa 350 B.C.
Némi, Sanctuary of Diana, Central Italy, Etruria
Bronze, fully cast, 50.5 cm
Former Tyskiewicz Collection, Br 321
Denon Pavilion, Ground floor, Room 20

PAGE 70
The Cat Goddess Bast
reign of Psamettic I (664-610 B.C.), 26th Dynasty
Bronze, blue glass, 27.6 cm x 20 cm
Sully Pavilion, Second Floor, Room 29

Male Mask
reign of Amenophis IV-Akehnaten
Plaster, 20 cm x 14,5 cm, E 27489
Sully Pavilion, Second Floor, Room 26

Execration figurines
13th-12th century B.C.
Terracotta, 14 cm, E 16492
Sully Pavilion, Ground floor, Room 18

PAGE 71
Warriors in a chariot
8th-5th century B.C.
Polychrome terracotta, Chypro-archaic
Aghia Barbara, MNB 391
Sully Pavilion, Ground floor, Room 21

PAGE 72
The God Bes
30th Dynasty, 379-341 B.C., Serapeum of Saqqara
Limestone, 92 cm x 62 cm x 28.5 cm
Sully Pavilion, Ground floor, Room 2

PAGE 73
Christ removed from the Cross
Burgundy, second quarter of the 12th century
Wood, with polychrome residue, 155 cm x 168 cm x 30 cm, RF 1082
Richelieu Pavilion, Ground floor, Room 2

PAGE 74
Attributed to Domenico of Paris
The dead Christ adored by John the Evangelist and Mary Magdelene
1470? Polychrome terracotta, 104 cm x 142 cm, RF 3003
Denon Pavilion Mezzanine, Study gallery 2

Joos Van Cleve
Christ as the Savior of the World
Circa 1516-1518
Oil on wood, 54 cm x 40 cm, RF 187
Richelieu Pavilion, 3rd floor, Room 9

After studying at the Angoulême comics art school, Nicolas De Crécy worked for two years with the French Walt Disney Studios. Meanwhile, he found the time to make the highly acclaimed album 'Foligatto', scripted by Alexios Tjoyas, which made De Crécy an instant success, garnering him many awards. He followed that with a trilogy starting with "Leon La Came", a satire of post-industrial society. Other prominent works include "The Celestial Bibendum", "Prosopopus," and he is presently in the middle of an absurdist anthropomorphic series called "Salvatore" (NBM). He has become famous as a mad genius, mixing fantasy, absurd humor and realism with breathtaking classically styled illustration, presenting a fresh original voice.